BECOMING A
TEACHERPRENEUR

Use The Skills
You Already Have
To Get Paid What
You're Worth

JARROD ROBINSON

with Andy Earle

For my teachers.

Table of Contents

Teaching for the Joy

After working with thousands of teachers across grade levels, subjects, and geographic locations here's what I've come to understand: **teachers are the most fundamental people in society, yet they are underappreciated and underpaid**. We expect teachers to work for the joy and satisfaction. But joy doesn't pay the bills and satisfaction doesn't put food on the table. If we don't start compensating educators more fairly, we're going to lose a generation of talented teachers, and with them, a generation of young minds. Thankfully, I've found a way for teachers to make extra money using the skills they already possess.

It's not only *possible* for teachers to earn a healthy wage doing what they love, it's easy. But not by operating the same way as everyone else. To make big money as a teacher, you have to think outside the box. I know some teachers who earn three or four times more than the average for their school. And some even earn ten or twenty times what their colleagues are making. I'm one of those teachers and dozens of others are my good friends.

A Teacherpreneur only earns part of their income from a school salary, they earn the rest of their money online by sharing their teachings with a global audience. They use the exact same skills, knowledge, and lesson plans they developed in the classroom to build digital income streams that pay out on a regular basis and grow steadily with each passing year. They don't just use innovative methods to teach students face-to-face, but they also search for creative ways to educate vast numbers of students through the internet, and monetize their teachings.

You're not a bad person for wanting to educate kids *and* make money. Aren't we supposed to be getting paid well for doing what we love? Isn't that success? Why should you have to live in poverty in order to love your job? Brain surgeons love their jobs too, but we pay them $600,000 a year and we pay teachers $60,000.

One study found up to ⅓ of teachers work second jobs outside the classroom to make ends meet. Software developers and teachers have the same education level but the wage disparity is huge. Why do we make teachers choose between a fulfilling career or a decent standard of living for their families?

The truth is you don't have to choose. You can have *both*. I've done it and I'll reveal exactly how in this book—plus I'll show you how to do the same.

My name is Jarrod Robinson, I'm a Physical Education teacher from Victoria, Australia. In 2008, I began blogging about my classroom happenings and other teachers found my tips and tricks useful. I grew my email list and client base, marketed my blog, and became known as the PE Geek. Currently, I run a company, manage several apps, and collaborate with teachers all around the world to build secondary revenue streams. *I decided to follow my passion.*

People avoid chasing their passions for any number of reasons. Some teachers feel nobody cares about their struggle, as if they are shouting into the void. Others tell themselves success only happens to a chosen few, so why bother?

No matter what your individual strengths are as a teacher, you can chase your passion and supplement your income. In the following pages, you'll learn all about the techniques I've used to build streams of passive income for teachers all around the globe. We will meet awesome, motivated people, hear all kinds of stories, and learn about secret histories... including:

- The story of Angry Birds, the most popular gaming app ever developed

- The psychological marketing tactics of the San Diego Zoo

- How the Rolling Stones inspired a generation of students to learn multiplication

- How an unknown rapper convinced the internet they were losers for not knowing his name

- And much more...

But first, we need to take a trip to Africa.

It's time to talk about poop!

CHAPTER 1

Removing Cardboard Hats

It's hard being a teacher today. Teachers are overworked, underappreciated, and overwhelmed. It's a highly skilled round-the-clock job that pays more like something a college student might do for the summer. Many talented people are leaving the profession because they can make more money, have more freedom, and feel more appreciated in other careers—and that's a huge loss to our schools and our kids.

Thankfully, I've found a way for teachers to do what they love and still provide a good life for themselves and their families. I've learned how to get paid handsomely as a teacher, without resorting to cheesy get-rich-quick schemes. I've discovered a way to take control of your time and career and I've taught these techniques to other teachers all over the world—with great success. In the pages that follow, I'll teach you too. But first, I want to tell you the most interesting scientific fact I know...

There is only one other animal on the planet, besides man, that can navigate by following the Milky Way. This particular creature is an insect famous for rolling around in it's own feces. At first glance, the Dung Beetle doesn't look like it has much going on underneath its 'shell,' but when researchers started to probe this dull bug they uncovered a host of impressive hidden abilities. It turns out the approach these researchers used is the exact same approach the best teachers take to uncover hidden abilities in struggling students.

It started with a simple observation: dung beetles navigate perfectly, even on cloudy, moonless nights. Researchers started to wonder how they were doing it. Were these bugs tapping into the earth's magnetic field to keep themselves on course? Did they use sound waves to track their flight path? Could they be aware of some mysterious new energy that defied modern science?

A team at the Johannesburg Planetarium had a theory. They wondered if the bugs might be using aspects of the night sky to find their way around, as seafaring merchants and explorers did for millennia. So the scientists set up a state-of-the-art dung-rolling racetrack in their dark dome theater and displayed a beautiful night sky with all the stars, planets, and moons removed. Only the Milky Way was visible. Even under this minimal night sky the beetles rolled their balls of dung across the table in perfectly straight lines.

The results suggested dung beetles are able to navigate at night by orienting themselves to the Milky Way. But this theory had never been put forth and the researchers wanted to do more testing before rushing off to publish their findings. They ran a second experiment in which they fashioned little cardboard hats for the dung beetles. The hats prevented the beetles from seeing the Milky Way and, sure enough, as a result, they wandered around aimlessly on the table.

The discovery of the navigation powers of the dung beetle has many parallels with teaching. Here are the three big ones:

1. Teachers like to tell you boring stuff in interesting ways.

2. People sometimes look down on teachers, but we're actually awesome.

3. It's a teacher's job to help students discover hidden abilities.

As teachers, we aim to help our students take off their cardboard hats and navigate through life.

Anne Sullivan taught Helen Keller to read and write even though the young girl could not hear, see, or speak. Instead of giving up on Keller, Sullivan saw her potential and helped her to reach it. For example, Anne spelled the word "water" on one of Helen's hands while pouring water on the other to teach her the relationship between the word and the object.

Anne figured out a unique way to take off Helen's cardboard hat. Through their partnership and friendship Helen and Anne became well-known for their lessons, revolutionizing education methods and collaborating with some of the most notable people of their day.

Another great teacher and exemplar of this creed is Father Greg Boyle, the founder of Homeboy Industries, a Los Angeles bakery that provides former gang members a fresh start in the world. Before he was a non-profit entrepreneur, and before he was a priest, Greg was a teacher. In his pivotal book, Tattoos on the Heart, he tells the story of his first day on the job, walking down the long hallway of Loyola High School in Downtown Los Angeles to teach his very first class.

The hallway seemed to go on forever and Greg's head was swimming with premonitions about his first teaching experience. He had no idea he was about to receive a piece of advice that he would follow for the rest of his life. Donna Wanland's door was open as he walked past and Greg knew she was a veteran teacher sure to be filled with sage wisdom. Donna was reading a book at her desk when he walked in. Her advice was straight to the point: "Know all their names by tomorrow. And it's more important that they know you, than they know what you know."

Donna's advice rings true across all levels of education, management, and business. When we educate anyone, the most important thing is to establish a connection. We must understand our students before we can help them grow into their best selves. We need to demonstrate that we value the student as a person, they can't feel like they are merely 'work' to us. It has to matter.

In a viral video from 2017, fifth grade teacher Barry White Jr. demonstrated a personalized handshake with every student in his class—plus a few outside of his tutelage. In the segment from ABC News, kids line up along a wall as Mr. White Jr., dressed in a crisp black suit, dishes out handshakes, salutes, foot taps, and high fives in a series of intricate patterns. White's energy brings their spirits up, readying them for the day ahead. Those students feel valued and cared for. That's what it takes to be exceptional at this. But we certainly don't pay the Barry Whites of the world as if their work really matters.

Teachers wear a lot of different hats. We are a listening ear for students in crisis, a resource for those looking to enhance their lives, and an advocate for those who need to be spoken up for.

Not everyone is cut out to be a teacher. We all know some 'teachers' who lazily hand out packets, sit behind their desks, and phone it in. And, of course, there's the ones who play movies every day. In my opinion, real teachers go above and beyond the bare minimum and sincerely invest in the wellbeing of their kids. Those are the teachers we desperately need more of. Those are the teachers who make a difference in the lives of their students.

If that sounds like you, I want to help you earn what you're worth as a teacher so you can live the life you want while doing what you love. The world needs more of you.

In a report from Business Insider, it was found that teachers in the United States spend roughly $500 of their own money on school related expenses each year. That's a troubling number when many of those teachers can expect to earn a salary of less than $40,000. For many teachers today it is a regular struggle to afford rent, food, and a comfortable way of life. Salaries for educators actually dropped by 4.5% over the past decade.

This is no way to treat the people who are shaping the minds of the next generation. Teachers today are stressed, underpaid, and uncertain about the future. As an Australian teacher myself, I know the experience of being underpaid and underappreciated is a worldwide issue. Teachers around the globe find themselves paying for their own materials while public schools face budget cuts and private tuition is on the rise.

In the 2019 PDK Poll of Public Schools, 71% of Americans reported believing teachers deserve to be paid more. The study also found 62% of teachers have considered leaving their jobs, with 55% saying they are ready to go on strike for higher wages. This frustration permeates all of our lives. As educators, we're expected to give our all for a system that doesn't see us as being worth the expense. Everyone wants change but no satisfactory solution has been proposed.

I'm not going to fix the broken education system but I have something that can help. I was able to find a set of proven tactics any teacher can use to supplement their income. This is not about getting a second job and stretching yourself thinner (even though many teachers do have a second job on top of their full-time career in order to make ends meet). I'm talking about another way.

I took off my cardboard hat, and now I'm shooting for the stars.

I became a Teacherpreneur. How I got there is an adventure in self-belief and chasing dreams. But my story also holds some useful how-to lessons for teachers everywhere.

My Teacherpreneur journey started with the sputtering screeches of dial-up during my senior year of high school...

CHAPTER 2

The Birth of a Teacherpreneur

Today, I'm known as the PE Geek. My company works with teachers to leverage their strengths. Through the monetization techniques you'll read about in this book, the project has become my full-time job and we employ a small team of people to manage everything now. But I didn't start out knowing this was what I wanted to do. My journey to becoming a Teacherpreneur began in earnest during my senior year of high school.

I was always interested in technology, spending hours in front of video games and screens. I kept up with the latest new consoles and arcade machines. But as soon as I experienced the Internet—even in the old dial-up days—I knew it was different. I was immediately hooked and wanted to learn everything about how it worked.

As part of a promotion, my family was given some free server space by our internet service provider (it was about 20 megabits). My parents didn't want it, so I decided to build a website. Back then, the internet was brand new and there were no 'rules' yet. People were experimenting with radically different styles of webpages. It was a brand new frontier and anyone could join. I learned to code HTML and built a website, and I did my high school senior project about teaching 18-year-olds to build websites of their own.

During this time, a teacher pulled me aside and said the sentence that would set me on my life's path: "Jarrod, you did a really good job explaining that to your classmates and seem to really light up when you're teaching." With this recognition, validation, and inspiration, I began to build my career around teaching. And the topic I wanted to cover was Physical Education.

A few years later, while I was working as a PE teacher, I realized something about technology that would change my life. It was Father's Day and I took my Dad and half-sister out to eat. My half-sister was only four years old at the time, but you would've guessed she was at least in grade school the way she handled her digital camera. She treated it almost like an extension of her own body.

At some point during the meal, she reached into her bag, pulled out her camera, and took a picture. Then she evaluated the photo by scrolling through her library of other pictures, determining her newest addition wasn't up to scratch, and using the delete command from the on-screen menu.

I sat there, watching her with a kind of awe I hadn't felt before. I too had been fascinated by technology growing up, but playing Donkey Kong was far less sophisticated than what my half-sister could do without a second thought. Until that moment, I never considered the limitless potential for technology to shape future generations.

Seeing my half-sister manipulate her camera so fluidly lit a fire in my mind: *this is the next generation of students entering our education system.* In only a few years, I would be teaching these children. I certainly didn't want to be using the same old methods we used before the digital age. It was time for a change.

I wanted to find something more powerful than traditional teaching methods. With new technology, I reasoned, the whole system could be reinvented and reinvigorated. And if I took action I could be at the forefront of this revolution.

The founders of Uber have described reaching a similar lightning bolt moment. After meeting at a conference in Paris in 2008, they were unable to catch a cab. Uber was born out of their frustration. Uber has defied criticism, the new way of thinking has triumphed over the old, and ride-hailing has come out on top. The company went public in 2019 for over $75 Billion.

Any innovation that changes the market is referred to as "disruptive." It's a term to describe a new way of doing things that is so far superior to the prior status quo it fundamentally alters the rules of the game. Disruptive technology allows for innovation, malleability, and flexibility in the economy. It pushes society forward.

However, people are creatures of habit. We prefer things to stay the same as they've always been. We resist change, underestimate its value, and sometimes even fear it.

In 1896, Parisians flocked into a theater to see Auguste and Louis Lumiere's L'Arrivée d'un train en gare de La Ciotat, (or Arrival of a Train at La Ciotat), not knowing they were about to witness the advent of modern media. As legend goes, the crowd was watching the screen when an image of a locomotive suddenly appeared, barreling toward them at top speed. Screaming, the patrons formed a stampede, charging toward the back of the theater to escape the oncoming train. A similar phenomenon plays out with virtually all new emerging technologies, from new vaccines to 5G telecommunication towers—the unknown frightens us.

Our fear of the unknown is largely irrational and can prevent us from making progress. While some educators might shy away from new technology or a teaching styles, the mavericks and early-adopters can be at an advantage. For example, as the world prepared for New Years back in 1999, the global media whipped everyone up into a frenzy about "Y2K." The world was on edge, waiting for machines to fail due to a universal coding bug. Many worried life as we knew it would never be the same.

It all stemmed from a theory computer calendars wouldn't be able to change to 2000. Banks feared interest rates would begin to calculate a 100-year minus rate. Tech companies and power plants feared shutdowns and shortages. Transportation systems worried their scheduling would be thrown off, leading to catastrophe. However, in the end, nothing happened. Computers functioned as they were supposed to and the world moved forward. Nowadays, massive computer bugs hardly make headlines.

In a similar way, some teachers are resistant to the use of innovative new educational technologies in their classrooms. Many are apprehensive about the ways technology can play a role in expanding their teaching efforts. This is especially true of older teachers who have been in the profession longer. But these fears are unfounded. In fact, technology is the biggest reason I'm able to help so many teachers. And it started very simple.

As Uber's founders were trying to catch a cab in Paris, I was getting into blogging. In those days, it felt like anyone with computer access had the opportunity to say something online and be heard. Blogging has been a launching pad for many teachers to turn their inner thoughts into fulfilling sources of side income.

I wasn't trying to become a celebrity when I started making content, I just wanted to keep doing what I've always been good at: tinkering with technology. When I came across Wordpress, I realized my students would benefit from having such a versatile and powerful tool at their disposal. I spread the idea of blogging through our classroom and found we had many opportunities.

In the first months, my students commented on my posts, created their own profiles, and shared content among themselves. Then we discovered a site that allowed them to upload sound files from their mobile phones directly to WordPress. From there it caught on like wildfire. We uploaded experiences from our trips and were able to do our classwork on the go. It inspired the kind of on-foot, outdoors content that forms the base of my work today.

While the students benefited from the experience, blogging was especially therapeutic for myself. Being able to reflect on each day, my students, and my actions made me feel good. I kept documenting my journey and encouraged others to pick up blogging as an educational and personal expression. I had no idea how many people read my words. I just wanted to share my life with the world.

Then, the first comment came. I booted up my computer and found an email from a person named Tim, who commented, "This is the truest and most brilliant blog post I've ever read." I couldn't believe it. Someone was reading my blog! I was ecstatic, and I attacked the process with renewed vigor. It felt incredible knowing my words were reaching those around me—and resonating. I had something valuable on my hands and I doubled down my efforts.

Many years later, I realized this comment came from a bot. It was a fake account. But by then it was too late; my site was already successful. That bot comment was exactly the encouragement I needed to get my business off the ground.

After a couple years of blogging, I was moderating a thriving community where I could discuss ideas and concepts with interesting people. My investment in technology was paying off.

My big opportunity for expansion came in the form of a bimonthly magazine based in Australia about physical activity and education. I started writing for "Active Education" and my audience blew up. My website started to see a lot of traffic. When the magazine folded unexpectedly, I was left with a stash of unpublished articles. So I decided to turn my words and teachings into an ebook. I compiled the articles, wrote an introduction and conclusion, and published the book on my website. Then I made a blog post with a link to the ebook. When I logged back in the next morning, 40 sales had been made. It was surreal and game-changing. I thought, *wow!* I could really get paid for what I was doing online...

I was able to get ahead of the curve by embracing technology. I monetized my teaching skills in ways I never imagined. Only a decade ago, I was a full-time Physical Education teacher. Now, I run a seven-figure online education business, help others launch businesses of their own, and go on new adventures every day.

Anyone with the drive to teach a class is more than capable of mimicking this success. I'm here to show you how to become a wildly successful Teacherpreneur. But first, what is a Teacherpreneur? And why am I so confident you can do it? Allow me to flatter you...

CHAPTER 3

You've Got This

I coined the phrase Teacherpreneur after realizing how similar entrepreneurs are to teachers. Teachers are lifelong learners. They are motivated, smart, passionate, and mission-driven. If you don't have grit and extremely thick skin this profession will chew you up and spit you out, like old gum under the edge of the desk.

To be a successful entrepreneur you need to be courageous, bold, and inspired. Success in one field doesn't necessarily equate with success in another, but the best teachers and entrepreneurs have many overlapping traits. If you can deliver great presentations, expand your knowledge, and shape young minds, you have all the skills you need to run a side business.

Jack Ma, the founder of the globally renowned Alibaba Group, worked as an English lecturer before launching his company, which now provides innovative tech solutions to millions of consumers. In 2016, Ma was listed among the wealthiest tech billionaires by Forbes. Some of Ma's success, undoubtedly, can be traced back to qualities he developed as a teacher. As an entrepreneur he has to invest in self-improvement, adapt to the market, cater to customers, take calculated risks, and learn at all times.

Here are the top 6 areas of business teachers can nail.

#1 Selling

Picture walking into a modern-day high school classroom. You stand in front of 40 teenagers, ready to teach something they aren't ready to learn. Their focus is divided, and in the battle for their attention, you're losing to social media. You must sell your lessons as useful, interesting, and worthwhile if you want to have any chance of making a connection or positive impact.

Students are impatient and effective teachers have to do more than recite from a textbook, they need to make the learning process engaging and meaningful. Your job isn't just spewing facts, it's inspiring students to believe in something. Research shows the most significant factor in student achievement is the quality of the teacher.

A great entrepreneur, Steve Jobs, had an almost mystical power to convince coworkers they could achieve the impossible. He sold everyone, from colleagues and investors to customers and family members, on revolutionary ideas and convinced them they could do better and should expect more.

The ability to sell an idea can often be more important than the quality of the idea itself. In 1975, Gary Dahl released the Pet Rock to the masses, which he'd invented after listening to his friends complain about cleaning up after their pets. Millions bought the worthless stones, turning Gary Dahl into a millionaire.

It wasn't the rock itself that made the product work but the box. Dahl packaged the rock in a cardboard box with a handle, airholes, and ardent instructions on how to best take care of the new pet. People got the joke and the pet rock became one of the most infamous pieces of marketing America has ever seen. Sales can be more important than the product itself.

Likewise, a teacher who can sell students on the idea of their own success is going to have more motivated students. If you can do that, you're on the right track.

#2 Communication

Success as an entrepreneur requires excellent communication skills, which most teachers have. Entrepreneurs need to present ideas to investors, make first impressions when networking, and instill confidence in employees, partners, and clients. They also need sharp conflict management, negotiation, and mediation skills. They must cater to demanding clients by focusing on the broader vision and letting go of ego.

Similarly, in the classroom, teachers create enthusiasm towards the subject and remove any inhibitions and fears students may have had. That's a form of sales. From incorporating teaching aids, such as video conferencing and computers, to dividing the class into small teams, teachers are always working to increase interaction and sell students on working together.

Teachers also have to cut through the influence of video games and social media to leave positive impressions in students' minds. That requires savvy communication skills.

#3 Fundraising

Raising money is almost synonymous with the word 'entrepreneur,' and teachers have this skill too. In the business world, capital helps to convert ideas into profitable companies. Likewise, exceptional teachers realize the importance of using all resources available. Public funding only covers the necessary things, but art projects, field trips, and sometimes even warm clothing for impoverished students aren't always in the budget.

Teachers need to leverage resources ranging from the school administration to parents and local business owners to provide students with the best experience. Teachers are always ready to look for contribution sources and are skilled at customizing their pitch to different audiences while highlighting the value of the proposal. Additionally, exceptional teachers often use their own money to supplement classroom resources. Several studies show most teachers, with very little fanfare, spend $500 per year to make sure their students have everything they need.

Teachers believe in their students and work hard to make sure they receive the adequate materials to further their development. In the same vein, entrepreneurs work hard to make sure their ideas come to fruition. This can only be accomplished with adequate funding.

#4 Knowing Your Audience

Understanding consumer behaviour is vital to any entrepreneur. By getting to know consumers better, businesses can target their campaigns, position themselves for future relevancy, and provide superior service. The same is true in the school systems. As teachers come to know students better they will be able to deliver content in ways the students understand and respond to. They'll learn to tailor their approach to suit the needs of every student.

In class, teachers must listen to the students and separate the griping from the honest feedback. We can't please everyone all the time, and we don't pander to every whim of our students. Similarly, a good entrepreneur is able to parse through information to find what is authentic and what is noise.

#5 Adaptability

While necessary in all professions, adaptability is especially important when working with non-like-minded individuals. One of the reasons attributed to the fall of Nokia was that the company failed to adapt. Through its rigidness in approaching an unfamiliar market, they fell behind and are now on the fringes (my students only know of them through jokes).

Successful entrepreneurs are willing to modify, improvise and switch their strategies as they continue learning more about their audience. Similarly, teachers know when they need to be flexible and work outside the prescribed curriculum.

In a classroom of 30 students, nearly half the kids may be bored or lost at any one time. You can get questions that take the lesson in a completely different direction than initially intended—not to mention other issues like budget cuts, sick kids, and snow days. My most memorable teachers are the ones who were able to roll with these disruptions and work them into the lesson flawlessly. I try to make sure my students recognize their ideas are valid and appreciated. Together, we build community. A Teacherpreneur knows when to adapt. There are no roadblocks, only different paths.

#6 Caring and Passion

Elon Musk cares deeply about the future of the planet and preventing climate change, so Tesla gives away its patents to other car companies to help promote the vision of more sustainable electric cars. This kind of passion and care for others is endemic to Teacherpreneurs. For most teachers, money is the last thing on our mind. We work because of an inner desire to improve students' lives. We work tirelessly to develop customized lesson plans and to always improve ourselves for the benefit of the kids.

An effective teacher is passionate and cares about seeing their kids succeed. Students feel this enthusiasm and it causes them to be more motivated in classroom activities.

You're Cut Out for Success!

When you got started as a teacher, you probably needed some help. But after a few years other teachers were coming to *you* for advice as assistance. Today the classroom is your dojo. Your skills have made you a formidable authority. If you wanted, you could sell anything to those students. Becoming a Teacherpreneur is about finding your next audience and making the sale.

In the next chapter, I'll tell you everything you need to know about sales to get your business moving...

CHAPTER 4

What We Can Learn From Angry Birds

Mikael Hed's company is responsible for one of the most popular mobile gaming apps of all time, and their success can be attributed to one of the oldest ideas in sales. Mikael's company, Rovio Gaming, is the creator of Angry Birds, a game that has become a cross-cultural phenomenon, recognizable all over the world (and making millions of dollars each year). The game sprang up from a simple drawing of a grouchy bird that one of the team members drew.

Since then, Angry Birds has exploded into multiple spinoff games, clothing lines, and two movies starring notable actors. There are many mobile games out there, but only one has franchised with Star Wars. The game itself is maddeningly simple. What set Rovio Gaming apart wasn't the product, it was their impeccable sales skills.They knew if they could sell a $1 product to a million people they would make a million bucks. They just had to convince a million people to spend a dollar.

Sales is about conviction, innovation, and connection. These are qualities all good teachers possess. Conviction comes from belief in the topic you're teaching. Innovation requires approaching problems in a new way. Connection is about figuring out what the other person wants and how to best provide it. Good teachers are natural salespeople, so there's nothing to be worried about as you get started becoming a Teacherpreneur. Rovio used these three qualities to rise to the top of the mobile gaming market, and you can use them too. However, Rovio's success would never have been possible if it weren't for the pioneers of the smartphone: Apple.

At the 2007 Macworld Keynote, Steve Jobs took the stage in his trademark black turtleneck and jeans, ready to shock the world. He looked out over the crowd and announced that the company was introducing three things: a new iPod, a revolutionary mobile phone, and a breakthrough internet communicator. He then repeated the three things he was bringing to the table. Then he said them again. And again. Slowly, the audience picked up on what he was saying, and cheers began to rise in the room. It wasn't three separate devices, it was all three in one. With the flourish of a magician, Steve Jobs unveiled the iPhone.

Apple has dominated the competition in the mobile phone industry by miles through revolutionary advertising and superior salesmanship. Even though other phones have more advanced features, the iPhone remains the favorite because it was created and sold by a man with conviction, innovation, and connection.

Jobs was a master of showmanship, exciting people to think outside the box. Unveiling the Mac computer in 1984, instead of going for a classic ad, Apple released a commercial showing thousands of clones watching a big screen that spewed prose. Then a runner hurled a sledgehammer through the massive projection's face, waking everyone up from their trance. What did this have to do with computers? I can't tell you. But it speaks to breaking the mold, thinking differently, and doing something new.

During these keynotes, Apple never said "Please, buy our product." All they had to do was reveal what they were coming out with and add the right flair. That's sales. The core that runs through Apple's whole company is conviction in their products. Apple operates with an attitude of "if you don't like it, we'll keep going and leave you behind," so people clamber over each other to be a part of the next big thing. That's the power of conviction.

There are many reasons why your students might be disgruntled, but there are also many ways to re engage them with conviction. Maybe your fifth graders aren't ready to handle math and are digging their heels in like stubborn mules. Maybe your seventh period history class is burnt out by the time they reach your room. Whatever the case, your students won't like everything you teach, so it's up to you to drum up excitement and motivate everyone. When you teach with conviction, you help your students see the importance of the lesson. You also inspire your students to feel confident in their abilities so they're excited to tackle tests and bring home an A+.

Conviction is also paramount in getting people to buy. If you have a side job as a tutor, you better have the conviction to say, "Not only am I a great tutor, but I will help your student achieve their highest GPA yet without having to pull teeth." That's sales.

During the unveiling of the iMac, Steve Jobs refused to open doors to the public until the computer was ready to be demonstrated. When the screen finally booted up, a smooth, calm voice said "hello" and the crowd went bananas. The iPhone was not the first of its kind, but it was the first to look utterly futuristic. What happened was a masterclass in thinking outside the box. A new twist on an old thing is sometimes all that's needed.

You could sell an online course about how to teach the state capitals to 5th graders. And if you package your course in a fresh, clean way with a single innovative quality, you might start making sales (more on how to do that later).

The third quality of a good salesperson is the ability to connect. Apple products have been flying off the shelves for years because consumers feel a connection with the company. The marketing speaks loud and clear and the brand has a positive message. They sell people on the elegance and sophistication of their products, along with the exceptional quality. Apple connects with their customers on a meaningful level.

How do Teacherpreneurs lock in that ability to communicate with our own audience? First, you have to actually listen to what your students (or clients) are saying. They're all different people with different interests and you have to reach each one differently. Being able to reach a variety of personality types is the backbone of any sales outreach. One way to do this is to focus on being personable and building relationships. People react to people, so you have to stop selling your product and begin selling yourself.

For many of us, the word 'sales' conjures up an image of a slick used car salesman, trying to peddle a spray-painted clunker with rust in the gas tank and sawdust in the engine. But this is a stereotype, and we need to break it down in order to succeed as Teacherpreneurs.

The best salespeople have an ability to connect with prospects, ask great questions, listen, and empathize. Being genuine will always win. People react poorly to false excitement or enthusiasm. Legitimate belief in the sincerity of your product is critical.

With so much conflict happening around them it's important for teachers to express themselves clearly and confidently. Great educators know how to get information across with ease and follow up with students who are struggling. The same practice is helpful with potential clients who are on the fence about a purchase decision. Practicing communication skills inside and outside the classroom will boost your ability to connect. With a stronger connection, you'll be more adept at tuning into what's working when you attempt to influence others.

Not every great salesperson is bombastic, just as not every teacher is a bubbly Zooey Deschanel or an awe-inspiring Robin Williams. Sales is scary. For many people the fear of rejection can be too much to handle. But it's nothing to lose sleep over.

You'll learn that when someone is saying "no" in a sales process, it's not personal, it's just business. They don't need what you have. Your product is not for everyone, and you shouldn't try to sell to people who are a bad fit because they won't like the product. It's actually good when people turn you down because it beats having them say yes and then leave you a bad review later on.

Understanding the motivations and desires of your students, staff, and customers will help your career as a Teacherpreneur. Just as with any discipline or skill, the more you practice the better you'll become. When you get into sales, give yourself permission to make mistakes and grow.

Get started. Practice hard. Don't give up.

CHAPTER 5

Finding Your Audience

Finding an audience of consumers and getting them to buy from you isn't as easy as finding a classroom. While every room is clearly marked with a room number and teachers and students are often assigned to one another, entrepreneurs have to seek out their audience. This search might feel unfamiliar or daunting, but it's straightforward if you follow three useful techniques:

1. Solving a problem

2. Studying a market

3. Being flexible to reach more people

An example of the first strategy, solving a problem, comes from 1965, in the locker rooms at the University of Florida. The assistant football coaches brought in a team of scientists to tackle a problem the Gators couldn't seem to shake. Practicing in the scorching Florida sun, players were collapsing from heat exposure.

The researchers tested players, ran drills, and measured everything from performance to dietary intake. They discovered the problem was a combination of drained fluids, electrolytes, and carbohydrates. They hoped their solution, a drink to replenish all three at once, would be a success.

They couldn't have been more right. By identifying and solving a specific problem, the University of Florida researchers were able to aid the Gators—and they created one of the most recognizable brands in the world of athletics: Gatorade.

They succeeded by executing the first strategy for identifying an audience: solve an existing problem. The players needed a way to acquire energy, resupply essential minerals, and maintain adequate hydration. Gatorade addressed all of these issues, replacing everything lost by the body while also tasting cool and refreshing.

After the introduction of Gatorade, Florida's football team could stand the blistering heat much better—and they rolled over their opponents that season. When they won the Orange Bowl they attributed the win to Gatorade. Over the next few years, sports teams all around the world began to supply Gatorade on the sidelines. A new tradition was born: at the end of a big game, players from the winning team drenched their coaches in the lemon-lime liquid.

Today, Gatorade is one of the biggest companies in sports, sponsoring everything from NBA superstars to local 5K events. The beverage's rise to glory demonstrates how identifying a need helps you discover an audience that's ready to buy your solution.

When becoming a Teacherpreneur, ask yourself what problem you solve and conduct research about your target consumers to find ways to reach them. One way to do this is by copying the pros. For example, if you want to start a teaching podcast, study other teaching podcasts to see how they attract listeners. Go to your competition's pages and read their reviews. What do people like? What do they dislike? How can you take advantage of these things? As Sun Tzu said, knowing your enemy is critical to success. While he was giving advice about war, the underlying knowledge still applies! Ask yourself, "How can I make my competitors' products better?"

Another strategy for finding your audience is to assess demand for your solution. While there is always going to be some competition in every market, too much might reduce your chances of success. If you are looking to sell children's books, aim for neighborhoods lacking youth bookstores or children's publishing companies. To find areas with high demand for children's books, keep an eye out for communities with higher birth rates or more schools per capita in addition to a dearth of bookstores. Concentrating on those places would significantly improve your outlook.

You can even research *yourself* to help find a market to sell to. Pinpoint something valuable you can teach that few people know how to do, such as how to deescalate classroom conflict, and suddenly you're a sought-after commodity. Find teachers struggling to manage rambunctious students, create a solution to help them, and *Boom!* there's your audience. The trick is to use market research rather than intuition. Look at what others are doing successfully, don't take advice from unqualified people. The more thoroughly you investigate, the more precisely you can target potential customers.

Elon Musk said being an entrepreneur is like chewing glass while looking into the abyss. This is not supposed to be easy work, but assessing the market before you start will save you time later on. Tesla, for example, makes affordable electric cars to reduce our impact on the environment by decreasing the carbon footprint of humankind. The market was hungry for Tesla's product because people wanted to help the Earth but weren't ready to stop driving. Tesla didn't create the desire, they just based their business on a need that already existed and wasn't being met.

In addition to solving existing problems and researching the market there is one more technique you can use to find an audience to sell to: adaptability. When Amazon began to dominate the bookstore market, Barnes & Noble was worried. However, B&N realized they had something Amazon didn't: physical locations. In a few years, Barnes & Noble rolled out bars and cafés in their stores to offer something Amazon couldn't. This helped the company to survive another day on the bookseller battlefront. If your market starts to turn in a new direction, you'd better react appropriately or else you'll be left behind. When your business is malleable, you can keep finding new ways to serve your consumers better.

Another example of using flexibility to grow an audience comes from rocket scientists. In 1982, Lonnie Johnson was attempting to build a heat-exchange pump for NASA when he encountered a fateful malfunction: the prototype sprang a leak and a jet of water shot across the room, splashing against the wall. Thousands of hours of work were wasted. But an idea sprang into Lonnie's head to build a high-performance water gun.

From his mishap, Johnson created one of the most popular toys of the 20th century: the Super Soaker. Lonnie Johnson was presented with a problem and chose to adapt rather than fight against it. This is a reminder to stay flexible and embrace change when starting a business. Fail to do that and you might lose out on a prime market. It's not rocket science!

If you don't adapt, your business can be dead in the water. After the outbreak of Covid-19, the world saw things cannot always operate the same way forever. Restaurants and bars found themselves closing down to focus on delivery or take-out options. Many businesses had to get creative to stay open. Movie theaters began selling popcorn by the trash bag. Gyms put up walls between treadmills.

My favorite story about restaurants during 2020 comes from Coquine in Portland, Oregon. The restaurant is a staple in SouthEast Portland, serving farm-to-table American food. After Covid-19 hit, and orders started to dip, the restaurant rolled out a new plan: selling uncooked ingredients for customers to cook themselves at home on their own schedules. The neighborhood got fresh, wholesome ingredients (literally "restaurant quality" food) and Coquine supported struggling farmers and helped out customers all at the same time.

Solving problems, studying markets, and maintaining adaptability are helpful techniques for positioning yourself to gain an audience, but you might have trouble analyzing which audience to target. How can you decide on the best candidates? A great trick for sorting through your options is to run a SWOT analysis, which stands for Strengths, Weakness, Opportunities, and Threats. Using the SWOT system, you can consider your choices honestly.

- **Strengths:** Your biggest advantages. What's the top benefit to using you over the competition? What special sauce can you bring?

- **Weaknesses:** The downsides to your approach. Where might this project come up short and how can you prepare for these possibilities ahead of time?

- **Opportunities**: Elements of your situation you might be able to take advantage of. Is the market promising? Is there a chance to improve?

- **Threats:** Aspects of the environment that can stand in the way of success. What are the risks and obstacles that might make things hard for you?

To demonstrate how this works, let's do a SWOT evaluation of tutoring as a possible entrepreneurial prospect.

Strengths: You have an advantage because you're already an educator of children. Being a teacher is synonymous with patience and childcare, so parents will look to you first. Also, you have a network. Parents are willing to recommend you to each other, and other teachers can vouch for your proficiency in your subject.

Weaknesses: If you feed off of the group energy of a classroom then individual sessions might grind your gears. Or maybe you don't have time on the weekends or evenings to be a reliable tutor.

Opportunities: Parents in your community are already looking for productive ways to fill their kids' time. You can access students around the world online who don't have many academic resources physically nearby, which is rewarding.

Threats: There might be an influx of tutors thanks to COVID, and it may be tough to find a way to stand out in the market. Make a plan to overcome these threats.

Through the SWOT analysis, you can determine whether a particular opportunity fits your criteria and puts you in a position to succeed.

Building your audience can sound hard, but there are ways to make it manageable. You can reach people to support your business if you solve their problems, research their markets, and adapt to suit challenges that arise. After you choose an audience, it's time to find clientele and form long-term business relationships. I'll cover that in the next chapter.

CHAPTER 6

The Importance of Listening

When rapper Lil Nas X came onto the music scene in 2019, his avant-garde blend of country and rap wasn't well received. But the hate didn't stop him from achieving success. It just meant conventional ways of attracting people to music wouldn't work for him. He had to come up with something new. And he ultimately did it by listening to his audience.

Lil Nas X made a name for himself with a song called "Old Town Road," using a viral marketing strategy: he made memes about his own song, pretending everyone else was talking about it, and flooded Twitter and Reddit. When people saw the memes, they didn't want to be out of the loop (we all want to want to fit in), so they flocked to the song en masse and Lil Nas X had his foot in the door.

The country music world wasn't ready to accept this meme lord with open arms just yet. In fact, many critics dismissed Old Town Road outright. They refused to believe a track involving rap could possibly be considered a country song. It was sacrilege!

This controversy gave Lil Nas X even more publicity, helping the song gain popularity. The more he stirred the pot, embraced memes, and leaned into what his audience wanted, the further he was able to ride the pop-culture wave to stardom. In fact, I first listened to his song after I heard the Country Music Awards were denouncing it as a joke. The world was curious what was causing all the commotion.

In this chapter we turn to the topic of listening to your audience. Meme marketing isn't the only way to see what your audience wants from you. But if you don't find some way to communicate with your audience, people won't connect with you or be into what you're selling. On the other hand, when you work to create a positive relationship with your audience, you will gain their faith and build a strong community who will buy your products.

When I started going around as the "PE Geek" online, I never expected the pseudonym to gain a following so massive it would change the course of my life. I only wanted to make a blog. As things grew, I grew personally at the same time.

Interacting with my audience helped me see my hard work materialize. It allowed me to read and hear how my efforts were making a difference in other people's lives, and to receive feedback that helped me improve my content and offerings. For these reasons and more, one piece of advice I always give new Teacherpreneurs is to start out with your mailing list.

An email list is one of the simplest and most effective ways to interact with your community and grow a positive relationship. **It is a collection of contact addresses provided to you willingly by potential customers and interested community members.** These are people who have asked you to inform them about your business and products. This list keeps you in contact with your patrons so you can update them with new offerings, updates, and content. A study from 2015 showed that 46% of businesses use email lists and invest in email marketing. Email has one of the highest investment-gains ratios of any marketing strategy in existence.

With an email list you can target people who have already shown interest in what you do. It takes the same amount of time and effort to send an email to one person as it does to a thousand. This gives you a way to regularly contact everyone in your web without requiring them to get any new software or devices.

Email might be old, but it's classic for a reason. And when combined with contemporary technology (CRM, automation, analytics, integrations...) it's one of the best tools at your disposal. A proper email list gives you three things: prospecting, lead conversion, and an easy way to retain customers.

If you had an email address back in the early 2000's you probably remember those wacky old chain emails people would add you to randomly.

- "Send this to ten people and a stranger will give you a free golden retriever!"

- "For every person you forward this to, Microsoft will give you $250.00!"

- "If you received this it means you are one of the prettiest girls! Send this to 10 people or you will be ugly for 10 years!"

Those emails were a cultural phenomenon and, as Lil Nas X proved, those can be turned into million-dollar marketing campaigns. Imagine advertising your service through an email chain. Wouldn't that be powerful? With the right kind of email marketing strategies, you can achieve that. Everyone who likes your email can forward it to a friend. If everyone sent an email "to 10 people," the message would circle the globe in minutes. One email can have long-lasting ramifications.

How does an email list enable strong communication? Having an email list is like bringing your whole audience together in one theater. It's like having a private research lab and your own massive subject pool to run studies and see what messaging works best. It's like a sounding board for your company! When you have an email list, you can talk to your customers directly, at zero cost.

All you need to get started is a list of emails, but you'll want a few other things as well in order to create a truly receptive audience. Listen to feedback and find out what keeps your customers engaged and receptive. The more receptive they are, the greater the responses and conversions your emails will generate. You want to build a personal community around one thing: the concept you are selling. Don't let your message get diluted.

Another point is that your list is yours. It's different from an audience managed by a third party (e.g. a social media network) as those are not actually owned by you. If anything happens with the network or your account gets shut down, your community is toast, but with an email list you own it forever and it's free to use.

- Through email you can connect with your users regardless of their device

- Email helps you nurture a steady flow of traffic to your website on command

- Most people in the world never delete their email address

- Email is one of the most direct ways to reach your audience

On my first website I gave away my eBook for free and it required visitors to enter their email address, but I didn't pay much attention to the small list of emails. Two years later the list had grown to about 1000 subscribers and I sent out an email to offer a discounted product. I made two sales from that first email and never looked back. I now have over 10,000 email subscribers who follow my updates.

Having an email list is the single biggest asset in my business. I work hard to provide quality content to help my email subscribers in whatever they are doing. Through my email list, I've been able to organise workshops in over 20 countries around the world. When people ask me how I get speaking gigs all around the world I say its simple, I have a quality email list. I send out an email asking if anyone is keen to host a workshop and I will get 100 emails back that day from 30 different countries offering to do an event.

I've also had a number of guests from my email list present webinars on my platform and come on one of my podcasts. These connections have opened multiple doors for me including a TEDx talk, a published book deal (which I am in the process of completing), and much more.

You don't build an email list overnight. It takes time, hard work, and love. But when you invest time in the people on your list you build a tribe that will help you achieve whatever you want. For me, it has allowed me to have 100's of yearly membership subscriptions to my ConnectedPE membership platform, as well as speak all over the world.

It doesn't take more effort to communicate with your entire audience than it does to communicate with one audience member. Interacting on a regular basis, even once a week, gives you access to valuable information to set your business on a path for ongoing success. Just don't get too sucked into your digital empire! In the next chapter, I'll share what I've learned about *balance*.

CHAPTER 7

Finding Balance

In the late 1990's, recent college grad Sara Blakely was learning the same lesson many new Teacherpreneurs come to grips with in the early days of their enterprises: maintaining a full-time career while starting a business isn't easy. Finding balance is a constant struggle.

Frustrated with a lack of comfortable pantyhose on the market, Sara crafted a few fruitless innovations before successfully macgyvering nylon tights into snug, footless leggings. Having never taken a business class, nor worked in fashion or retail, it seemed unlikely Sara would be able to produce and sell her leggings at scale without serious work. But she wanted to try.

First, Sara buried herself in developing her invention. The prototype took a year of nights and weekends to get right—on top of her regular 9-to-5 job selling fax machines. After struggling to balance her career with her side hustle Sara finally struck gold with one hosiery mill owner who ran the idea past his daughters. They loved it, Spanx was born, and Blakely became a billionaire. If she hadn't found a way to balance her day job with her passion project, she might have thrown in the towel well before hitting her big break.

There is often quite a bit of uncertainty when we start out as Teacherpreneurs. What if things go wrong? Is this a waste of time? Are you really the right person for this? Doubt can be paralyzing on Day 1 of any new entrepreneurial journey. Money is going to be tight during the first few months. For this reason, hang onto your job until the income from your side hustle is high enough to completely replace your salary. Many Teacherpreneurs never quit teaching. They just enjoy the extra challenge, community, and income they receive from running a side business.

According to a Business Insider article, around 43% of Americans have a supplementary source of income. But that doesn't mean it's easy.

Imagine you've just had a hectic day in the classroom and your lesson planning has fallen far behind where it should be, but the day's not over yet because it's time for your side hustle. At this moment, are you feeling excited, energized, and motivated? Or are you maybe feeling like you've just run a marathon only to find the elevator in your apartment block is broken and you'll have to take the stairs all the way to the thirteenth floor.

Teacherpreneurs are familiar with this second feeling.

Building a side hustle is no walk in the park. This must be a project of passion, something you see yourself committing to, rather than a half-hearted attempt to earn a few extra dollars. Balance is important during this phase. You need to take time for yourself.

When looking for balance, the first thing to do is define your purpose (I know, we're starting with the easy stuff). As you begin building your hustle, you have to look at it from all sides. This something you're going to put sustained energy toward for an extended period of time. If you get burnt out later on, circle back and repeat these steps again.

One of my friends, Aaron, was working in real estate finance doing menial, minimum-wage labor. But he was thrilled, because every night after work Aaron walked in the door, sat down, and started to write. His passion was poetry and storytelling. He found happiness in his craft and it provided an emotional contrast to his 9-to-5 job. It gave his life more meaning.

To stay inspired like Aaron, remind yourself why you are pursuing your side hustle. What will it give you that your day job doesn't? Is it about income? Does building a community excite you? Does it offer a creative challenge you're not getting at work? Or is it simply a way to explore your interests and passions? Without clarity of purpose, all the extra effort can start to drain you.

After identifying a purpose, decide whether to follow a proven framework or go off the beaten path. Both options can be right for different people at different times. In the past, I have taken my own way, working alongside others to build a more unconventional sort of empire. However, one time I worked within a sales letter template laid out for me and available in the community. I just plugged my information into the letter, made sure it was accurate, sent it out, and got a $10k deal within days.

Having a plan is imperative in order to keep moving toward your goal. Try breaking projects into components to gain a sense of control. Keep your milestones time-bound and realistic, being sure each is something you can actually do every day.

Try not to think of your day job and side hustle as independent. Instead, talk to your company about your side hustle. Establish clear expectations and highlight how one will enrich the other. There will always be lessons and skills from your day job that assist in your side hustle, and vice versa. You need to spot the crossovers. Think about how your current employer manages you. Through observation you can learn to better manage others and yourself. What resources does your company use that would be helpful in your side job?

When you're at work, you really do need to focus on work. If your side hustle can't support you independently, you don't want to risk your day job using company time to narrow down your new Twitter handle ideas. While your day job and passion project aren't mutually exclusive, you shouldn't double dip work hours with side hustle hours. Instead, you'll need to learn to divide your time.

Side hustlers don't get much of the tantalizing luxury we call "spare time." Teacherpreneurs should be prepared to squeeze their days for maximum productivity. When you're at work, teach fully. But when you're hustling... that's all you should be doing. Cut out the noise, silence the distractions, calm the wandering thoughts. Focus on your side hustle and get your work done. I recommend scheduling at least 10% of your most productive hours to your side hustle.

With such a packed schedule, don't forget to pencil in a water break. In fact, go get a drink right now and come back to this book. You might not have time again until tomorrow afternoon. I'll wait!

You're, back? Perfect! I hope you used that healthy break and light joke to get a head start on my next piece of advice—loosen up a little. No one wants their passion project to turn into another stressor to manage. Hustling is a lifestyle, not an obstacle to suffer through or "grind out." You need a long term strategy to destress, unwind, and evaluate whether everything's really under control.

Working my side hustle showed me the importance of maximizing every moment of the day. Rest is just as important as work and is a big part of a balanced lifestyle. Take advantage of quiet moments, write down what you are grateful for, and enjoy the story around you. Or play your favorite song and meditate. Maybe make time for your loved ones and share experiences together.

Take care of yourself too. Exhausting yourself to the point of burnout will make you unhappy and unhealthy. Plus, it will have a negative impact on the quality of your work. You'll be working harder to produce an inferior product. You wouldn't want your students or customers to have a bad experience because you're tired.

Sleep, drink water, eat vegetables, get your heart rate going, and get in shape. Importantly, listen to your body. What works best for you?

One recent study found athletes who followed an exercise program that matched their genetics experienced 600% greater gains than those who followed an exercise routine that was a poor fit for their bodies. Following similar diet and exercise habits to what your great, great, great, grandparents would have experienced is a good way to tailor your health habits to your body. Also, experiment. It helps to have a full bottle of water next to the bed so you can wake up hydrated, refreshed, and ready to go. Try starting off with some water in your system. It really works for me.

My final tip for finding balance is to evaluate the purpose of your project (again)! Déjà vu? Nope. You may have defined your purpose at the top of the chapter, but it can be easy to forget. The busier life gets, the more important it becomes to remind yourself why you started in the first place. Review, reevaluate, and redirect your mission constantly. If your purpose is misaligned with your efforts, you aren't doing yourself any favors.

CHAPTER 8

Tutored by a Man in a Barrel

One of the first places many teachers turn for side income is tutoring. Today, with families turning to online tutoring, there are more opportunities than ever for talented teachers to make money tutoring children from all over the world. And online tutoring is as simple as building a profile, setting an hourly rate, and watching the clients roll in. You can build up a significant level of income without ever leaving the comfort of your home.

In this chapter, I'll show you how online tutoring works and how to get started with it. But first, let's visit one of the very first tutors.

Diogenes lived thousands of years ago in Greece and was one of the original cynics. In those days, a cynic wasn't pessimistic. Ancient Greek cynics detested civilization and rejected the comforts of society. Diogenes lived in a barrel, naked, in the middle of a market. However, his genius rivaled the most famous philosophers.

A contemporary of Aristotle, Diogenes' approach was comically stark in contrast. For example, when someone asked Aristotle to define a human, he thought for a moment, then said "a featherless biped" (Aristotle was really fun at parties). Diogenes thought this was a dumb answer, and in response, burst into Aristotle's classroom holding a plucked, live chicken, threw it down, and yelled, "Behold! A man!" while the naked chicken stumbled around the room.

Unlike tutors of today, who meet clients at their homes or connect virtually, Diogenes could only be found on his barrel at the market. According to legend, the Macedonian king Alexander the Great once came to visit Diogenes there. Alexander wanted to speak with the philosopher after conquering Greece, to touch base before laying siege to the rest of the world. He came to the market, stood in front of the barrel, and asked Diogenes if there was anything he needed from the great ruler. Diogenes looked up at the King of the World and asked him, "Could you move aside? You're blocking the light."

So why did this smelly, pain-in-the-neck tutor endure throughout the ages? Because he made a lasting impact on his students and shaped their thinking. Diogenes found brilliant ways of teaching his ideas through action. His life demonstrates a world-changing tutor can come from *anywhere*. He taught Aristotle (and all of us) not to dismiss ideas simply because they come from a lunatic.

Today, tutoring can be done virtually. One of the most famous tutors of all time, Merlin the wizard, taught King Arthur to strategize by viewing ants and fish. Today, however, we possess a power even Merlin couldn't access: the magic of the internet. In the 21st century, its no longer necessary to be in the same room as a person to tutor them. In fact, in-person tutoring opportunities are limited; go digital to broaden your reach and earn more money.

The flexibility of the internet allows us to work almost anywhere in the world. With an internet connection, you can access your clients at any time, on the side. You can create a unique experience for yourself and your tutees. This is an evolving market, so you have the opportunity to get your foot in the door. While tutoring is not everyone's favorite role, it is accessible to anyone.

When you tutor you are no longer in front of a classroom. Instead, you are with a few students, or even just one. This means you have to connect on a more individual level. Take it back to basics. During one of my first tutoring gigs I worked with an inexperienced student. It wasn't like the classroom setting I was used to. Before he could learn anything, I had to get him to trust me.

When you tutor someone, they must know they can trust you. Think back to a class where you couldn't understand something. For me, it was pre-calculus during my Junior year of high school. I couldn't figure out derivatives. In a moment of kindness, one math teacher realized I was slipping and offered me tutoring on the side.

I stepped into her office for that first tutoring session feeling dumb and embarrassed. My friends were off playing and I was doing extra math. When I didn't immediately understand the first problem, I felt even worse about myself. All the attention was on me and it made me anxious. However, I trusted my tutor. She was patient and allowed me to voice my frustrations. I was able to be vulnerable in front of her and she let me know she was on my team. Trust is important in any partnership, especially tutoring.

My math teacher built strong trust by making sure I was on the same page as her and that I was always able to understand what she was saying. I was born with the brain of an athlete and a creative writer—I'm not built for math. She helped me develop tricks I could use to figure out the concepts. Everyone learns differently and once I trusted her, we were able to make huge strides together.

The final thing a student must have before they can make meaningful strides with a tutor is knowledge that progress is being made. At the end of a tutoring session, it's helpful to review the topics you covered. Make sure they know and understand the materials and are comfortable talking to you about what they do not know. Kids are stubborn. They don't like admitting they're wrong or don't understand. Make sure your students know their sessions are theirs and the focus is on their success, and that might mean getting uncomfortable.

It's more important that they know you than they know what you know. Connection before correction.

I'm not going to tell you how to tutor (that's what the internet is for--plus, you're already a teacher). Instead, I'm going to reveal how to build up a client base. Tutoring is in-demand and well-paid. Quality SAT tutors command anywhere from $45 to $300 per hour for instructing high schoolers on testing strategies and college preparatory content. Becoming certified requires effort but it's worth it. One-on-one tutoring with students can be a great way to make money, especially since you can source clients directly through your school. The key in marketing your services is to be unconventional. Stretch yourself.

There are many tutoring companies around the United States, most of which would love to bring a certified teacher onboard. This will consistently provide work and you won't have to go through the process of scheduling, marketing, or finding clients. Additionally, there will be some structure through the company and you'll have a team of other tutors to support you. The only reason I might suggest going an alternate route of finding clients yourself is it allows you to stand out and have more control over the process.

When you're thinking about new ways of finding clients, ask yourself who you could reach out to in your community with access to a large number of potential students. One avenue is to go through college professors. When you approach a college professor in a specific department they can advertise your services to their students. It can be as simple as going to your local university and putting up flyers on the announcement board. "My name is John Smith and I would love to tutor you in math!" Drum up attention.

Don't be afraid to show off. You want to attract attention. In the Amazon, birds grow bright colors and impressive plumages in order to attract mates. In a world full of sparrows, be a bird of paradise.

One great place to get started with online tutoring is a website called VIPkid, which allows you to tutor students from other countries virtually over the internet. This site specifically looks for people with teaching experience, a bachelors degree, and authorization to work in the U.S. or Canada. Additionally, you'll need to have a fast internet connection and reliable technology.

I've had the pleasure of working with a number of aspiring, novice, and seasoned Teacherpreneurs on their online tutoring journeys. These conversations have enabled me to crowdsource common problems. One of these frequent mistakes is concentrating too much energy in one place. Focusing solely on one channel can lead you to neglect everything else. If you leave yourself at the mercy of a specific platform then any changes to the platform could interrupt your capacity to earn revenue and drive traffic to your site or profile. Make sure your platforms are diversified and you have clients coming to you in multiple ways. Do email blasts, be active on social media, generate word of mouth, put up posters, and do anything else you can think of. Make sure the stream of new clients is always there.

The key to being a great tutor is to connect with your students and let them know you are on their team. Tutoring might not seem glamorous but even Alexander the Great, after being told to move out of the light by Diogenes, said that if he wasn't the king of the world, he would have liked to be the naked philosopher in the market. Imagine the freedom of controlling your own journey. Imagine telling the most powerful man alive to move aside because he's blocking your light. Tutoring can be your ticket to the Teacherpreneur life.

CHAPTER 9

Get Paid for what You Already Do

The next method for supplementing your income as an educator is like an online potluck for teachers. Everyone brings something to share. Except, instead of food and drinks we bring digital educational resources like lesson plans, worksheets, class activities, and test question banks. Other teachers who want to use your stuff in their classrooms can pay you a few dollars for the rights. I know many teachers who regularly earn a few thousand dollars per month in passive income from this approach.

One of the most important keys to making this digital potluck work for you is something I learned from a regular potluck I attended years back. It started ordinarily enough, with an email inviting all teachers to join in a feast where we would each bring a dish to share with the group.

Normally a potluck host will send out a list of potential side dishes and ask guests to each sign up for one. This time, however, our host decided to leave it to fate and let people bring whatever they wanted. Imagine the surprise when every guest—over twenty people—showed up with bread rolls.

Yes, bread is certainly a smorgasbord staple, but variety is the key to a good potluck—and it's also the key to selling your lesson plans successfully as a teacher. If everyone shows up with the same stuff, it's not going to work. You've got to bring something new to the table.

Grading rubrics are like the bread rolls of the education world: every teacher has a drawer full of old rubrics, but that doesn't mean we should all go start posting them online. The reason we ended up with 20 baskets of bread at that potluck was because we were all thinking in terms of what would be the easiest thing to bring, not what would be unique and exceptional. When you're looking to sell your goods online, this is critical. The internet doesn't need more rubrics unless yours is somehow spectacular.

A platform I use is **Teachers Paying Teachers.** The program provides a way for teachers across all levels of education to build their classroom content and passive income. New teachers use TPT to purchase pre-made resources from other more experienced educators, freeing up some time as they learn the ropes of a new subject. Even seasoned teachers often surf TPT to find the freshest pop culture references, hip classroom activities, and hilarious Zoom backgrounds to keep students engaged.

Perhaps the most attractive aspect of this website is that you won't just be supplementing your classroom with fresh and diverse content by participating in TPT, you'll also be supplementing your income. As a budding Teacherpreneur, you can upload your favorite lectures, reference pages, or Roman history *Jeopardy!* quiz questions and know there's a teacher out there who would gladly send you a few bucks for a download.

As you use the program, you will earn money selling materials you only had to make once. If you're feeling underappreciated or underpaid for your skills as an educator, watching your sales rack up is a great way to see the value of your work.

You have a lot to offer other educators. Many gaps need to be filled in terms of effective and efficient resources for teachers. That's why there are over three million resources on the site! Here's some more data to give you an idea of how many educators are already using Teachers Pay Teachers:

- More that 67% of teachers in the United States use TPT

- 3 million resources are available on the site

- Over 1 billion downloads of resources have occurred

- Five million teachers used TPT in 2019 alone

Jen Regan, a fourth grade teacher and mother of three, found herself looking for extra income when she was on maternity leave for her fourth child. After giving birth to her son in January of 2016, she turned her attention to creating materials for Teachers Pay Teachers and blogging on her own website.

Today, Jen's best-selling product is her Growth Mindset pack, which is made up of ten lessons and activities to introduce students to the growth mindset in the classroom. This product is versatile and can be used across grade levels. Jen also has the Close Reading bundle which includes reading passages detailing high-interest topics. This helps teachers save time when preparing class material for close readings and responses. Jen has also created her own set of writing standards and uploaded it to TPT to help other teachers who might not have writing curricula available at their institutions. Through her perseverance, she created her own side hustle that operates alongside her classroom career.

Jen recommends finding your niche and making sure you actively contribute quality products to TPT. You can't cut corners. Especially as a new or part-time Teacherpreneur, you do not want to gain the reputation as someone who delivers low-quality products. If you do not give your full effort, you will get lost in the shuffle. Jen also advises connecting with other Teacherpreneurs, especially when you're just starting out. Making honest and genuine connections is crucial in business today.

Additionally, Jen advises that you give your resources as much exposure as possible so people can find them. Being present on social media is critical for pushing your product. Pinterest is an especially good resource as teachers use the platform to search for the latest in education trends, exchange ideas, and look for resources.

This is a terrific way to show off your resources and introduce potential clients to the brand. Invest time and effort in your first impression. Look for what makes you stand out to others. This is not a get-rich-quick scheme, but a long-term solution to help you passively supplement your income.

Step-by-Step Guide

When I talk about this platform, teachers often ask me to explain it one step at a time. I want to point out that TPT isn't the only online marketplace for teachers out there, it's just the biggest one and I've seen a lot of teachers do well using it, so that's why I recommend it. I'm not affiliated with TPT and I don't make money from referring you there. Feel free to apply this advice to another service. The information is transferable to multiple systems. But for the sake of simplicity, I'm going to walk you through using TPT.

First, create an account. On TPT, schools or coalitions of homeschooling parents can set up group accounts to get in on shared resources. Regardless, every user will need a personal account as well. TPT and similar platforms offer a standard commission for free accounts and a higher commission with lower fees for Premium Seller accounts (which costs about $60 as of writing this book). I suggest upgrading to the Premium Seller account as soon as it becomes financially viable because the switch can put exponentially more money in your pocket in the long run.

Once you've got your resources uploaded, you can set prices and let the platform take care of the rest. TPT handles the processing of orders and manages much of the customer support. The site will assign your store a unique URL so people can find you easily. Then you can market your page all over the internet.

One way to get noticed is by sharing your story and experience. When you connect with your audience by revealing your teaching history, personal journey, and the reasons why you're on TPT in the first place, you'll gain credibility. Once you have a good reputation, you can use events like flash sales to keep customers coming back for more. You should update your products, prices, and profile often.

If you ever feel lost or like you're not getting the most out of your platform, try visiting their in-house help service. Teachers Paying Teachers has TPT University, which is full of tips and tricks on how to optimize your account. You'll learn everything about creating resources and pricing them effectively.

The last thing to know about these platforms is their ability to record achievements. Teachers Paying Teachers, for example, keeps track of your milestones, making it easy to measure how far you've come in your entrepreneurship. I looked back on my own progress recently and saw my sales have been steadily increasing every year. Your success depends on your activity level. Now that I have become more established I'm comfortable taking my foot off the gas a bit, but the most successful online gigs translate to the amount of effort put in. Your passion and commitment will shine through and lead to exponential growth!

When you get started, it's easy to believe your resources might not be worth much, but don't get discouraged. You have something unique to offer and people are looking for it! The world's largest auction site was created when the founders posted online that they were selling a broken laser pointer and it was bought almost immediately. When they reached out to the buyer to ask why he wanted the item, he said he collected broken laser pointers. They realized one man's trash is another man's treasure and eBay was born.

One of the most beautiful parts about platforms like TPT is the vast community that comes built in. On these marketplaces, other people act as mentors instead of competitors. Rather than placing all your focus on selling your own products, remember to enjoy the wonderful resources, stories, and relationships of the Teacherpreneurs around you. They will help you avoid bumps in the road so you can progress more smoothly. By connecting and collaborating, you can be sure you won't be the twentieth person to arrive at the potluck holding bread rolls.

CHAPTER 10

Author an eBook

When the Amazon Kindle was released in 2007 it sold out within five and a half hours. The device ushered in an era of accessibility where busy readers can grab a copy of their favorite book instantly, without having to visit a bookstore. By 2010, thanks in large part to the popularity of the Kindle, ebook sales surpassed $1 billion and this reading modality become a mainstay in American culture. In 2019, eBooks generated over $2 billion in revenue. While traditional traditional books still have a significant edge ($22.6 billion in 2019), eBooks are a viable alternative for many readers. Their ease in transport, clean design, and linkable content make them perfect for the consumer on the go. eBooks can reach many people as they are viewable on readers such as the Kindle as well as laptops, phones, or tablets. Plus, they're convenient, with adjustable font sizes.

eBooks are also one of the most profitable and manageable ways for teachers to produce income on the side. As eBooks gain popularity, they are easier and more convenient to self publish than ever before.

In sports, when someone is "in the zone," they are performing way above normal and they almost can't be stopped. There are moments in Barcelona football games, when Lionel Messi gets that look in his eye that says, "nothing will stop me." Sabrina Ionescu, the all time leading scorer in NCAA Women's Basketball, will move *differently* than anyone else out there. These athletes are finding the zone.

When I wrote my first book, *Technology and Physical Education*, I was in the zone. Not because I loved writing the book itself, but because I loved my topic. Words flowed out of me and onto the page and I was sharing ideas I found interesting and important. I have a lot of respect for rabbits, but I wouldn't have been in the zone writing about rabbits. When you find your zone, you will know the ease of sharing your craft.

I learned a few important lessons while writing my book that I think are essential for every new author to know:

1. Clarify your audience.

2. Proofread like a pro.

3. Promote, promote, promote!

Follow these steps and you're on your way to eBook success.

Visit the Amazon Kindle store and take a look at the popular categories for eBooks, poke around on Reddit and other forum sites, and sleuth out what your crowd wants to see.

It might sound tricky to do "market research" as a busy teacher, but it's fun once you get the hang of it. Don't just skim the gushing 5/5 reviews, because negativity can be your friend too. Reading what unhappy customers have said about others' work can show you what people are looking for so you can fill the gaps. I've found the 3/5 star reviews often contain gold nuggets, as they tell you what the audience liked and didn't like. This way, you'll know what to accentuate in your own work. Listen to what readers are saying and figure out what they are looking for.

Don't get so immersed in research that you never put pen to paper, or fingers to keys. Allocate a set amount of time for research (e.g., 2 weeks, or 30 hours) then get moving. This will help you complete the necessary background work while keeping you from wandering adrift and waking up in a mire of facts that don't really add to your content.

Narrow the circle until you're left with your core source material. Also, try not to limit yourself to articles and blogs. Establish links to other books and eBooks, especially those with credibility among your audience already. This gives your work more authority and prestige. To do that, read the books on your topic.

When you're done researching, always check your facts. One piece of false information can ruin your reputation as an author and a businessperson, which is why proofreading is so important. This is the most important phase of the eBook process. Get feedback on your initial draft from as many readers as possible. Even proofreaders who know nothing about the topic can be helpful. Clarity, structure, and proper grammar will make you sound like an expert even if you're pulling your facts and stories out of thin air.

A poorly written eBook makes the reader question whether the author has any clue what they're talking about, even if it's coming from a genius! eBooks are easy to return for a full refund—customers don't have to mail anything back to Amazon. They simply click the "give-me-my-money-back" button. And if you don't proofread your book carefully before launching, that's exactly what's going to happen. They'll also click the "leave-a-1-star-review" button, which is even worse for you in the long run.

Don't be that author. The professional appearance of your work is imperative to its success. Poor grammar and improper punctuation can ruin your audience's experience. Hire an expert to proofread your work so there are no errors or awkward phrasing. Use their expertise to format your work for maximum appeal. When I wrote my first book, I made sure to have multiple objective readers look through it. I only chose people who were comfortable giving me tough criticism.

Before you jump into writing your first draft, it's a good idea to start with a full outline of every chapter. However, if you wish to free flow for the first draft, that is effective for some people. Just anticipate a hefty phase of rewriting after your first draft is completed if you go with this method. Whichever strategy you choose, pay respect to common rules and conventions:

- Split your eBook into several distinct chapters with different titles. This improves the organization of the book. It's safer to have too many chapters than too few!

- Use add-ins like internal links, bullet point lists, and mind maps, to spice up your content and make your eBook easier to understand.

An advantage of eBooks compared to traditional publishing is that when you write an ebook you can utilize add-ins to enhance and supplement the content. You'll be able to provide methods and examples that your readers can access quickly, creating a more thorough educational experience.

One piece many first-time writers tend to undervalue is the visual aesthetic of the book. Customers will judge your book by it's cover. They will utilize the "look inside this book" button. You could have the most brilliant insights in the world but without killer cover art and proper typesetting nobody is going to read it.

Formatting your book isn't something that has to be expensive or time consuming. For example, Open Office allows for quick conversion of .doc files into PDFs. It hosts a wide range of attractive fonts for you to choose from. And the program is completely free. Writing an eBook doesn't require technical skill.

Drop in an image or two.

- Explore the internet stock photography markets for proper photos that will make an impact, in accordance with your text's purpose, and won't get you sued.

- Stick to images categorized as "royalty free" and always be sure to credit the photographer in the caption.

- If you're looking for something particular, you might even want to hire a photographer for a half-day shoot. Depending on the photos you need, it might be the least expensive option.

- Avoid photos you've taken yourself, as they'll look amateur.

- The only situation in which personal photos should be used is when they have historical or personal value and contribute to the content of your eBook.

- For example, before and after pictures are always a great addition, even if you took them yourself.

Once you've finished your manuscript, selected your visuals, and laid everything out it's time to publish! Your audience is going to eat this ebook up once they catch wind of its helpful, thorough, and authentic approach. They just don't know it's out there yet. How do you make sure your book stands out among the others and gets in front of as many people as possible? Get on soapboxes.

Great **promotion** is essential to making your eBook a success. You don't need to search the Yellow Pages for vacant billboard space to promote your eBook, you already have a few awesome outreach tools available to you. You have a built-in audience through your niche, so get involved in the online community for your chosen field. Tell your friends about your new book. Write guest posts on industry blogs, run a few Google and Facebook ads, and employ social media to give your book a distinct advantage over the others. Whatever promotional methods you decide to employ, make sure you never stop telling people about your book—the more the merrier! Persistence is part of making sales.

Appear on relevant podcasts to talk about your book. This offers you a platform to make your pitch straight to your audience. If you're writing about college advice for prospective students, appear on some education, parenting, or teen-related podcasts to share your advice with listeners who will value it (one of my favorites is the Talking to Teens podcast). There are many awesome podcasts out there and you'll be able to find one in your niche that's thrilled to have you on to promote your book, share your opinion, and provide content to their audience. Everyone wins!

Make sure your book is financially friendly. The price should be in the right ballpark for customers to say, "Yes!" But you don't want to give out your eBook for free either. It's important to ensure you get the right value for your efforts in writing it. After a few people read your book they might start recommending it to friends and family. This doesn't mean you should stop promoting your book, rather it demonstrates how far-reaching your promotional campaigns can be when they lead to organic word-of-mouth.

You might be collecting checks on your eBook for decades if you create content your audience is hungry for, proofread to perfection, and execute a solid promotion plan at the right price. Everything else you do as a writer comes down to your personal technique and creating content that won't seem dated in a few years. The final advice I can give is my own personal list of writing tips:

- Never start at the beginning. The beginnings and endings of books need to hint at everything in the middle, while also being punchy and drawing the reader in. That's very difficult to do straight off the bat, and usually leads to a creative dead end. Instead, start directly with the body of the eBook and go from there.

- Don't jump head-first into writing. Plan, research, prepare, and focus. Starting impulsively usually ends the way it began.

- Don't say everything at once. Choose one aspect of your topic and write with that as the guiding principle. Otherwise, you'll just have a bulky, messy, loosely-connected piece of writing that offers value to no one.

- Designate a set part of each day for writing. Only writing when you feel inspired isn't realistic. Writing is tough work with ups and downs. The most important thing is to stay productive and on schedule!

Those are my best tips on writing an eBook. Not all of us want to be writers though. Some Teacherpreneurs are better at the podium or on stage than we are at the keyboard. If that's you, pay attention to this next chapter...

CHAPTER 11

From Teacher to Public Speaker

Some teachers have an ability to control a room. When these teachers enter a classroom (or dinner party), heads turn and people listen. They could be reading the side effects of a new heart medication and it would sound entertaining and valuable. If you're one of those teachers, you have something in common with Tony Robbins. And, as his situation demonstrates, it can be worth a lot of money.

Tony grew up in North Hollywood in a neighborhood he has (only half-jokingly) referred to as the "wrong side of the tracks." His mother was an addict and physically abusive, so Tony pushed himself to become a protector, caregiver, and provider for his two siblings. But he felt trapped. One day, after ending his shift as a janitor, the 17-year-old Robbins visited a family friend and raised a question that would alter the course of his life.

"My dad said you used to be a loser," Tony told the man. "How come you're so successful now?"

"If you wanna be successful," the man replied, "go to a Jim Rohn seminar."

Robbins spent his entire check on a Jim Rohn ticket, and it paid off. Within a matter of weeks, Robbins was working as a promoter for Jim's motivational speeches while absorbing everything he could about the industry. Tony had found his mentor.

Jim must've seen something special in Tony. It might have been his warm, genuine, and confident demeanor. Or maybe it was the sense of maturity and leadership he developed while acting as the "father figure" of his household. Or it might have been the fact that Tony was a towering, 6'7" teenager!

Either way, Robbins was called to become a public speaker—and, thankfully, people wanted to listen. After years of work, Tony became one of the most influential speakers in the world. He empowers his audiences to tear down any obstacles in their way. And teachers can create the same sense of empowerment!

As a teacher, you are a natural public speaker, trained at keeping students engaged. You know how to make information personal to your audience, tapping into an emotional vein that a textbook could never reach. Public speaking is a lot like taking your classroom on the road, and make supplemental income.

One of the cruxes of public speaking is finding an audience. Be on the lookout for your first opportunity. It might happen next time a conference comes to town. These types of opportunities are common; when events happen, the organizer will put out a call for proposals. All you have to do is be prepared.

The first opportunity I had to speak was 2009, right before technology and Physical Education intersected, when nobody was talking about this possibility. I submitted my proposal, thinking I wouldn't hear back, but within a month I was slated to speak. Even though I didn't have much credibility, I was willing to put myself out there. When you raise your hand, you create opportunities for yourself.

Public speaking can seem challenging and intimidating. You might be an introvert who dreads the big stage. Maybe a class of 30 children is different from a lecture hall of 100+. This chapter is still relevant because everyone can benefit from honing their speaking skills. Every Teacherpreneur looking to expand their business will have to stand in front of an audience and sell at some point, even if it's just to film a video telling your followers to check out your latest product. Therefore, this chapter is going to focus on how to give the most engaging presentation you have ever given!

#1 The Hook

Great public speakers employ a story to capture attention and draw their audience in from the very beginning. You may have noticed me employing this method throughout my writing as well, because I want to make sure you are engaged. Remember the dung beetle? Sara Blakely founding Spanx? Lil Nas X's marketing? I used these stories to get you interested.

Make sure you do the same with your audience! Let your personality shine through in your words. That's what people want to see and what will separate you from other speakers, so don't be afraid to have fun designing your hooks and lead-ins.

#2 Outline

Part of writing a great speech is outlining its structure ahead of time so the presentation is easy to follow and remember. Think about how you wrote persuasive essays in school. Framing your speech around a thesis is crucial. With an outline, you can see how each piece of evidence relates back to the point you're trying to make. Make sure to bring back the opening story in some way at the end of your speech (in the last paragraph). This brings a sense of closure and completeness and prompts the audience to clap.

#3 You Catch More Bees with Honey...

Getting someone to listen to a speech is kind of like getting someone to eat a microwaved steak. Sure, it has the same nutritional content, but it lacks the sizzle. To get people to listen, you have to make your content appetizing! If you find yourself stumped trying to make topics like multiplication and conjunctions sound more appealing, lend your ear to this:

In the early 1970's, an ad agent named David McCall met with a musician named Bob Dorough to reinvent multiplication tables. On a trip in Wyoming, McCall had noticed his son knew all the words to Rolling Stones songs but wasn't able to memorize multiplication tables. He approached Dorough, a jazz pianist, to figure out a way to educate children through song. After a few weeks flipping through his daughter's schoolbooks, Dorough created "Three is a Magic Number," a song about math. A *good* song about math.

The musician and ad agent were onto something huge: a palatable way to teach boring stuff to children. So *Schoolhouse Rock* was born. The series ran for seven seasons on ABC, teaching kids about everything from conjunctions ("Conjunction Junction, What's Your Function?") to the American government system ("I'm just a Bill"). Schoolhouse Rock remains a staple of the American education system, with generations of children humming along.

In the same way that Bob Dorough used songs to get kids to pay attention, you can use stories with your adult listeners. Show what makes your topic fun and why you love it. Your personality and passion will shine through!

#4 Building Your Stage Persona

Public speaking is educational theater. Shakespeare said "all the world's a stage," and we can take this idea to heart when presenting to a crowd. A stage persona is essential. I don't naturally like being the center of attention. When I'm on stage I imagine I'm a different version of myself. *How does this Jarrod behave? What does this Jarrod do differently? How does this Jarrod react?*

Using this mentality, I can imagine a clean division between who I am in my personal life and who I am publicly. Yet, I have also found the qualities I love in "Stage Jarrod" have slowly transitioned into my normal life. I've found confidence, purpose, and drive in my day-to-day activities, which I attribute to public speaking.

It's also important to consider your "stage attire." When you're up on stage, being comfortable with your appearance goes a long way. Wear something appropriate but not restricting, an outfit that puts a spring in your step. You want to command the room.

#5 Remember to listen

Public speaking relies on making a connection with the audience. Receiving feedback can make your speech better. Call-and-response or dialogue also allows audience members to participate in your lecture. People love to speak up. By finding ways to include the audience in your talk, you give them that chance.

#6 Nerves of Steel

I sometimes still get freaked out when I'm getting ready to speak in public, even after all this time. One of my big fears is that I will accidentally say a curse word or something off-color and undermine my credibility. Before I go onstage today I take a few minutes of silence to assume the mentality of a teacher and leader.

Achieving a high level confidence took me a long time, but in the end it was worth it. I had to slog through a lot of nervousness to get here. I hate those moments when a conversation dies down and you're caught standing there awkwardly, staring at another person... That can also be what it feels like up on stage; the nervousness floods in. Your body's fight-or-flight reactions begin to engage.

Anxiety's worst enemy is preparation. Review your notes and practice your speech without them, so you always know what to say next. Practice with a camera or friend. Rehearse the speech until it is ready for the public. When the adrenaline rush comes, make sure you ride the wave, don't let it overtake you. You're going to do great!

#7 Finish Strong!

At the end of your speech, take a moment to remind everyone about the main points you just told them and why the topic is so important. You also want to make sure to reference the opening story again during your conclusion. And don't forget to tell your audience what you want them to do next (like follow you on social media, buy your book, or register for your free online training).

Here's an example...

The advice in this chapter can help you hone your public speaking skills and launch your career as a speaker. If you're serious about becoming a speaker, it helps to find a mentor who is already doing it to get you started. Tony Robbins found Jim Rohn. Find someone who can help you, choose a topic you're interested in, and start getting people fired up! You can use your ability to influence those around you and become known as an expert in your field.

But maybe you're more of an introvert and public speaking isn't a good fit. Or perhaps you're looking to build passive income that doesn't require you to travel, write speeches, and be "on" whenever someone hires you. In that case, have you ever thought about creating an app? It's not as tough as you might think. Read the next chapter to find out how I do it.

CHAPTER 12

Pretty Sure There's An App For That

I know dozens of teachers who own smartphone apps that generate hundreds, thousands, and even tens of thousands of dollars per month in passive income. You don't have to be a programmer (or hire one) to build an app; if you can imagine something, there is a very easy way to make it with the tools available today.

If you've ever taken some time to peruse the iTunes or Android app store, you're aware there is an app for everything. Most of us can hardly remember a time where we navigated without Google Maps, jogged without tracking our heart rate, or sat down at a restaurant without checking in to leave a review. And when we teach, the possibilities for software integration are endless. Technology continues to dominate the cutting edge of education as students stay up to date with the latest in digital study tools.

As a Teacherpreneur, it's crucial to consider how apps and software can assist your life. They can organize your clients, take and make payments, and keep track of your money. Apps have allowed us in the business world to become mobile and flexible with what our businesses are able to do. Through harnessing the software behind the new app world, you'll jump ahead of many others attempting to find success in the same market.

Mobile apps are incredibly profitable, with some of my most popular apps receiving hundreds of thousands of downloads. After starting as a side hustle, my apps have generated over $500k for my business. Being quick to take advantage of revolutionary platforms like apps and Wordpress has changed my life.

The market economy behind apps is powerful. About a decade ago, Pete Charette, a physical education specialist, was looking to build an app for his program, Power PE. The program was already a successful website that provided games, activities, and worksheets to help teachers make sure their students were active and healthy throughout the day. After retiring, Pete wanted to develop the program from a website into an app.

According to theappmatch.com, Pete's app has been a huge success, with over 900 downloads in the first month and another 600 during his promotional tour. Through the app, Pete says he is able to get his materials to people he never could reach before. Nothing beats apps in terms of ease, convenience, and streamline-ability.

Pete's story is not unique, and it's an example of how we are able to reach out to teachers on an individual basis. As an alternative, your app might be targeted at the students themselves. Kids are on the forefront of the shift into learning via technology. Adults often complain about how younger generations are always on their phones; what if we harnessed that power instead of dismissing its potential?

Those who can teach effectively through an app will become successful. In 2009, Carnegie Mellon University professor Luis von Ahn was inspired to create a program that served two purposes at once: teaching users a foreign language while also translating simple phrases in documents. Although the second feature was removed, he hit upon a great idea with an educational app accessible to anyone attempting to learn a new language. Born in Guatemala, von Ahn saw how difficult it was for people to learn English. Believing that "free education will really change the world," von Ahn and his team developed Duolingo to massive success.

Duolingo has exploded to become a successful product. Thousands have been able to learn a language by playing games and taking quizzes accompanied by cartoons—all while choosing time durations from five minutes to an hour per day. The app is simple enough for kids while not being patronizing to adults, and the cartoon owl has become a cultural staple.

The owl pops up as a notification on your phone with pithy comments about how you have not studied yet. Students love it and have even developed memes about being "terrified" of the owl discovering they haven't studied for the day. The app is free so Duolingo has become a staple in schools for language homework and supplemental education.

Harnessing the power of educational apps is one of the most direct ways to reach students and produce a side hustle. Launching a profitable mobile app can seem daunting, but you can launch an app and begin seeing profits within five days. This is the story of how I produced Loop It, my gif-making app:

1. The first step was to decide on a problem my audience would appreciate an app solution for. This required me to understand the challenges and obstacles they faced. While this might be more difficult for those outside of a given niche, its easy when you're one of the target users.

2. With a few ideas floating around my head, I jumped onto the website 'Code Canyon' & started browsing through their full application templates for iPhone/iPad. It wasn't long before I stumbled across a prime candidate I could repurpose to help solve one of the audiences challenges: 'Gif Factory', priced at $105 for an extended license. Using these templates enabled me to shortcut development by getting me most of the way towards my end goal. All I had to do was make modifications to

the branding and re-skin some of the User interface so it didn't look identical to the original template.

3. It was up to me to decide on an appropriate name and color scheme that suited my existing product line. I decided on 'Loop It', given the looping nature of animated GIFs.

4. After acquiring the source file, I downloaded it and hired a iOS Developer on Fiverr. While I certainly wouldn't advocate building large projects with developers from this platform, a quick re-skin is well within their capacity.

5. I made an order for the re-skin, a test version of the app and final submission to the app store. To speed things up I added a 24 hour turnaround for these items.

6. Within 12 hours I received the test version of the application with the changes I'd requested to the 'Loop It' Branding.

7. After completing some initial testing and producing a teaser video for social media, I was ready to submit to the iTunes App store, which was handled by the developer I hired on Fiverr.

8. Within 48 hours I received an email from Apple letting me know they had reviewed the application and Loop It was available for download. Now it was time to begin promoting the app to my network. The first thing I did was to go to social media and post on all my platforms, letting people know I'd made an app, what it did, and who it was available for. Following that, I made a blog post announcing the launch to my followers who might not be so inclined to use social media.

9. The final piece of the promotional puzzle was to run a competition which encouraged users to download the app and leave a review in exchange for a chance to win a $100 prize. It cost me $100, but I was able to generate over 47 entries with mainly 5 star reviews for the app, boosting it in the rankings and further

encouraging organic downloads. Nothing hits an audience like a strong user testimonial. People love connecting with others!

In the end, the total cost to release and market the app came out to $245, and we sold 313 units and earned $634 within a few days. With this style of launch I have proven many times across different styles of apps that anyone, regardless of experience, can produce their own app to serve an audience's needs.

Even with their ease of development, convenience, and smooth use, apps are often overlooked by many businesses, big and small. Many focus on a website, thinking it is more essential. While I agree websites are important, apps are more convenient and have many advantages over conventional websites. While there are an unlimited number of websites on the internet (with more being created all the time), apps are regulated and must be approved.

Think about the last five times you used your phone. Did you open a mobile site or did you go to an app? Research shows the majority of people flock to apps rather than sites; opening YouTube with one click is easier than dancing all over the internet in search of the right link. Additionally, as internet access is not guaranteed at all times, people may wish to use your app offline (or at least some features). This way, customers will be able to see your work even when they aren't connected.

People aren't likely to delete an app after downloading it, even if they have not used it in months. And as life inevitably changes in the future, people may rediscover your app at some point down the road when they have more time or different interests.

According to Techcrunch.com, the global app economy should reach $6.3 trillion by 2021, with 3.4 billion smartphones around the world using apps every day. As a society we are accustomed to using apps as almost second nature by this point. Hopping on this wave is a terrific way to generate revenue, income, and attention.

CHAPTER 13

Step Into the Digital Classroom

Creating online courses requires similar skills to the ones you already excel at and practice daily in your classroom. It's the most natural way for Teacherpreneurs to make passive income. An online course is any learning environment people can find and attend through the internet. The e-learning market is huge, and is poised to grow to roughly $398.15 Billion by 2026—so this is a prime sector of the economy to jump into. If you're not used to creating online content, you might have a few questions:

- Can I really do this?

- Why would people pay for my course?

- Do I have something interesting to say?

The answer is yes. Even if you don't have a background in business or video production there are resources to help turn your passion and knowledge into an online course.

One of the best things about developing an online course is that once it is recorded, **the work is done**. Courses allow you to put an asset in your shop that never runs out of stock. Your level of effort after that is entirely up to you. You could go on a promotional tour, investigate ad space, and build partnerships to gain exposure, or you could just post links to your courses in a few prominent places and wait for the students to roll in.

Another benefit of online courses is that you might inspire **positive change.** If you create a course targeted at teachers on how to get students more engaged, those teachers may learn something valuable to transform their own classrooms. Your course can make a difference. Your impact might spread to other schools and lead to positive change beyond the reach of your digital classroom. Plus, you might get free promotion from your fans!

Speaking of fans, another benefit of courses is inbuilt audiences. eLearning platforms are full of people looking for their next tidbit, so your courses can expose you to millions of potential new consumers. You can focus on creating better products, rather than spending your time building an audience for yourself.

Courses are also **adaptable**. During 2020's Covid-19 pandemic, many turned to online courses to bolster their knowledge and pass the time. Teachers with online courses around topics like homeschooling and remote classrooms saw sales increase by well over 1000% during the Covid-19 pandemic. Produce a wide variety of courses so you'll always have a hot topic, no matter what is trending.

Kelli Alaina found success by developing a course based on what people wanted to learn about, and listening to criticism from her customers. Her first product was an online mini course she put together after polling her social media following and discovering they wanted more information on leveraging Instagram for business. She developed a course and launched a 25-day free challenge, which attracted attention and drew followers.

"The challenge was a great way for my tribe to rally around each other as a community and enjoy the experience together," Kelly said. The project "created a lot of buzz and generated great testimonials. When I launched the course directly after the challenge, lots of people were eager to join the program right away." **Selling the course for $19, she made over $2,000 in two days from teachers looking to expand their social media networks.**

Following this success, she launched Stand Out Brand Camp, a course for Teacherpreneurs to learn marketing for social media. **Kelli taught others how to build business plans, message clearly, and develop marketing strategies.** Through her contact list and the attention from her free challenge Kelli filled her program to capacity, bringing in $15,000 before even completing Brand Camp. After adjusting the Camp according to feedback, she generated $55,000+ within its eight-month beta period.

Ask your **audience**! Just like Kelli, you have an audience somewhere. Find out what they want to learn about. Their feedback can help you decide where to focus your time and energy.

You have something to offer the world and you're working against yourself and those who might learn from you by keeping your knowledge inside! You are a *teacher*. You have no reason not to be teaching an online course.

We can learn a lot about online courses from the founder of iPhys-Ed.com, **Nathan Horne**. Nathan was a Physical Education teacher, but now his career is devoted to helping others share their purposeful teaching experiences. With a passion for traveling and for teaching in unusual situations, Nathan was destined to create a course. He admits there was a learning curve to get started. Today, however, his course is simple to update and maintain.

Nathan heard feedback from his readership and clients that other teachers wanted to use the presentations he'd developed. He jumped on the opportunity and built courses on iPhys-Ed.

The challenge Nathan ran across was pricing. In fact, pricing seems to be a challenge for many small business owners. Nathan's original price for his course was low. After receiving some advice from me, however, he decided his *Creating Game Animations using Keynote* course would go for $29.99. Cheap isn't always good. A lower price may cause clients to perceive your product as low value. That would be the opposite of what Nathan provides.

Getting started is simple. Just film some videos and plug them into an eLearning platform to host your course. These websites are user-friendly and easy to navigate.

How to Get Started

There are many ways to approach developing and launching an online course, but what's worked for me and the Teacherpreneurs I've trained is to decide on a general topic first. Make it something broad enough you can easily develop multiple courses within this area without getting bored or running out of things to say. For instance, my topic is how teachers can make money on the side.

- What are the topics that your friends are always asking you for your opinions about?

- Are there certain issues you have become known as an expert in?

You might be the person everyone goes to for recipes, financial advice, workout tips, questions about outer space, or any other random topic. Most people have some areas of expertise they aren't aware of. Teachers are especially likely to be asked for information and advice frequently.

Once you've narrowed in on a topic, browse through a dozen of the leading e-learning platforms and register for a handful of courses in your chosen topic area. Spend some time working through these to get a feel for what you like and dislike about each of the potential platforms (you're going to have to choose one). Also, this will give you a sense of what content already exists and what your competition is doing so you can be sure to provide something new and different when you make your own course.

The next step after you choose a platform and spy on your competitors is to generate a list of the most frequently asked questions people have about your topic. Head over to forum websites like Quora, eHow, Reddit, and YahooAnswers where people ask questions. Spend some time tracking down questions relevant to the course you want to make.

Next, select the most frequent questions from the list, organize them into a logical sequence, point a camera at yourself, and get a friend to ask you the questions one at a time. As a general rule, you want to find a total of 200 questions. Then you should cut it down to about 100 by getting rid of similar and boring ones. Group these into 10-15 groups of 6-12 questions each, and those will become the lessons of your course. Spend a few minutes answering each question on camera. It will take one day to film the course. I use a basic webcam for this and have never had any issues.

After the filming is complete, edit your course. You don't have to do it yourself. Video editors can be hired on a per project basis for reasonable rates. I use a firm based in India and they are exceptional. I get the videos transcribed into a single document then I go through and highlight which sentences to keep and which ones to remove. I generally don't do any reorganizing, since I already outlined the course before I started. My editors send me finished videos in about 2 days, complete with title animations, music cues, and transitions. I watch the videos and if I notice any small errors they fix it right away. As soon as I approve the files and pay, they deliver the videos digitally to me. That costs $180.

With your edited videos in hand, head back to whichever eLearning platform you liked best. Create an instructor account and start uploading your videos. Write a description for the course and for each lesson, find some images to make it all look nice, and create some quiz questions to test students' knowledge at the end of each lesson and at the end of the course.

Next, simply press the publish button, wait for your course to be reviewed and approved by the platform, and start marketing.

CHAPTER 14

Helping Others to Get Paid

Facebook and Instagram can operate without charging users because they make their money through advertising. In 2019, roughly 98.5% of Facebook's revenue came from serving up ads to their audience of over 500 million people. This simple formula generated $69.7 billion—more than enough to keep the company afloat and at the top of the technology world.

Advertisements are one of the most profitable ways to make money online. To pull it off, all you need is an audience. A website with visitors will work just fine. Or an Instagram or Pinterest account can be used if you have a following there.

Some might take offense at the idea of using advertising to gain revenue. However, if you are legitimately in favor of a product there's nothing wrong with promoting it. If you have a blog, podcast, YouTube channel, or any kind of media stream you are already promoting many different things whether you realize it or not. We constantly reference brands, products, books, apps, and websites, so we might as well be getting paid for it.

When you establish a partnership with a company, you approach a territory known as affiliate marketing. Before I mention anything else about this, I need to drill home a point:

Affiliate Marketing is **not** a pyramid scheme. It's a low-friction way to get started generating side income that doesn't require you to create your own product. Affiliate Marketing is a great way to build side revenue streams overnight if you have an audience. If not, start building an audience as soon as possible. Having someone to market to makes all the strategies in this book more effective.

The idea behind affiliate marketing is that you will promote another person's product to your audience. Imagine you are a language teacher with a following of individuals who are working on their language skills. You could create a product to help these people learn a language (e.g., flash cards, an app, a workbook, etc.) but that might be time consuming. On the other hand, you could partner with an existing company that already has a product (e.g., Duolingo). Once you start posting special traceable links to the Duolinguo app, they will pay you every time someone signs up. You'll start earning additional income and your affiliate partners will receive traffic from a trusted source. You're becoming a billboard with a pulse!

The most important part about affiliate marketing is trust. The products you promote have to be legitimately useful to your audience. Stick to promoting things you believe in and have tried. If you push products that are useless, your audience will see through it and stop following you. The difference between those who receive a bad reputation through affiliate marketing and those who are well respected is that the latter endorse products they use and like.

This process is not one where you are going to be retiring early, moving to Fiji, and living on your affiliate income alone—the amount of people who are able to pull that off is very low. However, affiliate marketing can start supplementing your income and adding hundreds of dollars per month in passive cash flow to your financial picture. If you already have an audience around you, this method pays for itself quickly. It's a great way to build upon the quirks of your specific audience.

At my company, The PE Geek, we work through the App Store and use the iTunes Affiliate Program. We started sharing apps and tools with our audience that we thought were useful for teachers. Whenever anyone signed up for an app within 24 hours of us recommending it we would earn a small commission (about 5%). That doesn't equate too much, especially when an app costs $.99, but it adds up and allows us to promote an app we know our audience will find helpful.

Promoting someone else's product doesn't have to be as direct as saying, "I like this product and you should buy it." Sometimes you can be more subtle and non-intrusive. Notice how Facebook's ads fit organically into the content on your walls. People spend countless hours on YouTube. When the ad comes up before the video, with the skip feature, you only have to watch for five seconds. Some ads last fifteen seconds. Then, during the video, the influencers often mention the sponsoring product as well.

While these kinds of ads are not overwhelming and can be moved through quickly, there is a numbers game being played. If 10,000 people watch the video, at least a few will want the product. Put an ad on your app and let money come through. As ads appear, especially those relevant to your audience's interests, you will generate a terrific passive income stream.

While affiliate marketing is an indirect way to generate income, you can also make some side money by working as a virtual assistant. There, you'll have the ability to leverage your time in service to someone else. These positions are flexible and often lucrative. Whatever your specific skill is, sites like Upwork or Fiverr can connect you with people who need your talents. You'll be able to create a profile and advertise yourself to others who may need your abilities. Doing so can even be very enjoyable.

Let's say you're an art teacher (and a good artist). You could list a gig on one of these sites and people would start to purchase your talent. You can do the work in your off time without interfering with your regular life. The same goes for music teachers, who might produce a jingle, soundtrack, or podcast intro. Whatever kind of skills you have can be advertised on these gig sites and it's an easy way to get started. You could go there right now and create a profile listing the things you are passionate and skillful around, and people will start hiring you.

Teachers are well-equipped to be virtual assistants. You already have tech savviness from the classroom. You have the time and ability to communicate with people across various mediums. You have months off over the summer, holidays, and weekends. Additionally, you are a quick learner. How many times have you been up the night before a lecture, learning all you can about a topic so that you can teach it properly to your students the next day? Most teachers can get themselves immersed in a topic quickly. There's nothing stopping you from being a highly paid virtual assistant, even in a space that has nothing to do with education!

Take the skills that make you a good teacher, like researching, organization, speaking, and communication, and roll them into another role as a virtual assistant. When you start posting on these sites, you never know where you might end up working!

In my businesses, I am always looking to hire virtual assistants with teaching experience to help produce content. Teachers have the most adaptable skill set on the planet. Through hiring teachers, our education business has grown very successful.

Nicole Morgan, a full-time elementary school librarian, says being a teacher and virtual assistant allows her to use her strengths. The role offers her flexibility in her schedule and a chance to do something different. Teachers don't get an off-day ever, we're always on the go and working a rigid schedule. Being a virtual assistant allows Nicole to complete tasks in her moments of down time.

You may love your class to pieces, but this side hustle gives you the opportunity to do something unrelated to them for a bit. We are all able to do our jobs better when we have an outside hobby. One of my friends is in finance and goes on a twenty mile bike ride every night to explore his city. These little moments enhance our lives, giving us the shot of serotonin we need to keep going!

Being a virtual assistant can come in many different forms. You can stay in the teaching field, perhaps grading papers for a professor. You could branch out to something else completely, like research for an author as they write a nonfiction book. You could scout basketball games at night. This is a varied field that will allow you to immerse yourself deep in your interests for supplemental pay! Affiliate marketing and virtual assistant gigs can be terrific ways to make money on the side. They can generate more than enough revenue to pad your pockets and give you a nice cushion to come back to at the end of the day.

CHAPTER 15

The Membership Economy

Amazon, Spotify, Verizon, and Comcast aren't the only ones who can enroll customers in monthly or yearly plans. Memberships are everywhere. In the world of live professional sports you can either purchase a single ticket or a season ticket. The difference in price is astronomical. A single game might start at $50 while a season ticket could be more like $8,000. However, the season ticket holder receives perks regular ticket holders don't have access to, like meeting the players, autographed jerseys, tours of the stadium, and other things exclusively reserved for those who commit to supporting the team.

Memberships are sometimes viewed as extravagant or wasteful but they are just a way for organizations to incentivize people to commit. Once we get a taste of the season-ticket life, it can be hard to go back to the single-ticket life. Scalable membership programs can open up avenues and doors.

When you buy a membership at the San Diego Zoo (as of 2020), you are presented with two options, the Annual Pass or the Keeper's Club. Those who choose the Annual Pass receive:

- Unlimited admission to the San Diego Zoo and the San Diego Zoo Safari Park for one full year

- Two 50% Off Discount Admission Coupons for guests

- Unlimited Africa Tram at the Safari Park

- Unlimited Skyfari aerial tram at the Zoo

- ZOONOOZ magazine subscription

- Exclusive Member specials

Those who purchase the Keeper's Club Membership receive:

- All the benefits of the Annual Pass

- Unlimited Bus Tours at the Zoo

- Free parking at the Safari Park (save $15 each visit)

- Exclusive Member specials

- Special early hours at the Zoo - In recognition of your contribution and participation in the Keeper's Club, you're invited to enter the zoo early from 8 to 9 a.m. the second Saturday of each month.

- Early admission to the Safari Park - On four Saturdays of the year, you can enter the Park before the general public. This opportunity is only available to members like you and it's available at no additional cost to you.

- Wild Perks™: Show your membership card and get 10% off food, merchandise and more!

With this scalable system, the Zoo does something clever: incentivize members to go further. Annual Pass members have the satisfaction of being in the "club," yet the Keeper's Club still has more to offer, tantalizing the Annual Pass holders into upgrading, and doubling their yearly contribution.

The Zoo is using something I call the "Large Coke Model." Their annual pass costs roughly twice as much as a single-day zoo ticket. *For double the money you get unlimited visits.* I call it the Large Coke Model because in the grocery store the smallest size of soda is often priced only marginally lower than the largest size, making us think we are getting the biggest bang for our buck by upgrading. I remember in primary school thinking I'd outsmarted the company by getting so much more for nearly nothing. But, of course, they knew what they were doing. They got me to hand over more change.

With an annual membership priced at roughly twice the cost of a single ticket, the San Diego Zoo asks customers to take a gamble: *do you think you're going to come back to the Zoo again this year?* If so, you'd be silly not to buy the membership.

Think about Spotify's model. The music streaming service launched in 2008 and has quickly grown to become one of the biggest names in the music and app worlds simultaneously. iTunes had a monopoly on the market for a decade, selling songs individually to the consumer. However, Spotify came in with a two-tiered model that circumvented this process: free or premium.

Spotify Free has unlimited music, but is peppered with advertising, suffers from a lower quality of sound, and does not allow users to listen without a connection to the internet. Spotify Premium, on the other hand, is high quality music without any ads, plus the ability to listen offline and create playlists, along with other benefits. The two systems work in tandem, solving individual problems. Spotify Free asks the listener "do you want to keep paying for music or listen for free?" The user wants the unlimited music, so they switch. Following up on this, Spotify Premium says "you like this, right, but the ads are kind of annoying. How about you pay $9.99 per month for no ads and better quality?" People find even more benefits to the service and Spotify makes money either way, off the Premium price (which is still less than buying six songs on iTunes) or the ads.

Teachers can create membership programs by introducing a recurring benefits schedule. Through these programs, you'll share access to new resources every day, week, or month and charge them an ongoing fee to stay subscribed. This allows for a long-term commitment. You'll have to keep coming up with great new stuff so members are incentivized to stay in the program.

Jocelyn and Shane are teachers who built a membership program as their side hustle. Out of Kentucky, Shane was a social science teacher and football coach while Jocelyn was an elementary school librarian. They currently work a ten hour week and bring home $50,000 per month (roughly $625 per hour)! They grew their annual earnings to seven digits in a few years through clever maneuvering and hard work. They did not use a get-rich-quick scheme. This is legitimate work that can pay off immensely.

Jocelyn and Shane were in their early thirties with two young kids to raise, a stiff teaching schedule, and a low income that limited their lifestyle. They knew they had something to offer: years of teaching experience others would find useful. They developed a program, *Elementary Librarian Community*, an online membership-based community packed with lesson plans and other resources that save thousands of hours of work. Jocelyn says, "My members are elementary school librarians from all over the world!"

Her best advice is to "add value." Jocelyn stresses that providing customers with value is one of the most important steps in driving traffic to the site. Through social media, she entices people to check out the website, where they realize the benefits that come from committing to a full membership. Nobody wants to be sold to. In the end, your product should sell itself.

This is not easy. "Be prepared to work a lot in the beginning," the couple says. "Take advantage of summers, days off, and evenings to batch as much work as possible so you can get ahead and won't be too stressed out when your schedule gets busier. You must plan times to work on your online business and even schedule backup times to work when life gets in the way. You cannot succeed in online business without constantly taking action!"

What set Jocelyn and Shane apart from many others was their commitment to listening to their customers; they wanted to offer a great experience. One of the best parts of membership is customer feedback. With membership programs, the consumer knows you rely on them. Patreon, developed in 2013, is a membership-based program that allows creators and artists to earn a monthly income by providing content for their subscribers, who finance their work. If someone is making a comic book and needs funding, they can reach out on Patreon, find supporters, and begin making work. In return, members receive special benefits from the artist.

When PE teacher Carl Condliffe created the My Study Series, he was following his passion for "flipped learning," an idea suggesting lectures be moved outside of class time in order to have students establish a baseline of concepts before coming to class (For example, the students might learn about the French Revolution before class then the teacher could hone in on the role Robespierre played in the Jacobian party). Condliffe is a big advocate of this type of learning, and realized his passion could be monetized as a side hustle. Thus, *My Study Series* was born: a platform with video content for students, allowing them to set learning goals. Each video has a quiz to test understanding. In essence, it gamifies learning.

Currently, Condliffe's income is from schools who purchase subscriptions to the My Study Series service. While a lot of work went into the project, Carl found the success of his membership program could be boiled down to three points:

1. **Set high expectations for yourself and your product:** Carl says it took time to realise just how valuable his knowledge could be – it's common to underestimate your own value. Aim high, and expect the best from yourself and your product.

2. **Work hard:** After the product launched in 2017, Carl estimated that about 1000 hours had gone into the product. He worked

every day until 1am to realize his dream, saying, "There are no shortcuts." Make time for the things you have to do.

3. **Look after your family first:** If you have a side gig that demands you work hard and long hours, your family will feel this the most. Carl says it's important to make time for the people you love; hobbies and relationships will give you the strength to push through and achieve your dreams!

While membership programs can seem daunting due to their upkeep, they bring together community like almost nothing else. Through your program, you'll be able to hear from your fans, learn what they are looking for, and tailor the service to their desires.

CHAPTER 16

What's Next?

You now know about all of the best ways for teachers to make money online and supplement their income. So what are you going to do next? Choose some of these strategies that resonate with you and start building your audience. No matter how you decide to monetize your teachings, an audience will be paramount.

Clarify your audience so that your research will be focused and precise. The quality of your subscribers will improve exponentially, your passion will resonate, and your readers will love it. Here are some questions you can ask yourself to make sure you fully understand your audience:

- If my audience were grouped together, what would the group be called? (eg. Teachers? Engineers? Startup entrepreneurs?)

- How old is my audience?

- How active is my audience online?

- What is the income level of my audience?

- What motivates my audience?

- What does my audience read?

- What does my audience already know about this topic?

- Where does my audience hang out online?

If your audience is made up of people like you, many of these questions can be answered through self-reflection. Think about what you like and dislike when you read or hear someone talk about your topic. Ask yourself whether you would subscribe to your own email list and follow yourself on Insta. Be honest with yourself about this.

One popular strategy to boost engagement and gain subscribers when you don't have any following at all is to do a giveaway. That's what David Dobrik did when he collaborated with SeatGeek in 2019. A few days before Christmas the immensely popular YouTube content creator posted an Instagram photo that set the world on fire.

"Hey guys! For Christmas, SeatGeek and I are giving away this Tesla to one of y'all! Just follow me and SeatGeek, share it to your story, and tag a friend in the comments! Choosing the winner on Christmas Eve!"

SeatGeek gained over a million Instagram followers in an hour.

Dobrik announced the winner on Christmas Eve and both he and SeatGeek were able to attract insane levels of attention online. People from all walks of life were captivated by the free Tesla and flocked to the page. While not all of us have the audience to rack up 4.5 million likes on our posts, this example shows that a giveaway can cause your numbers to skyrocket.

Using this strategy Dobrik boosted his own profile, along with Seatgeek's. Additionally, the media picked up on his outrageous use of social media and syndicated the campaign to an even greater viewership. Millions of people started tagging friends, following both companies, and flooding their websites with traffic. The car may have cost $40,000, but the attention worth the Tesla's weight in gold.

Whether you market via social media or email, interacting with an audience online is an incredible resource for feedback, community building, and emotional validation for what you're doing. Sharing and listening through mass media contributes to a positive relationship between teacher and student, or entrepreneur and consumer.

In addition to getting started on your audience, my second tip is to recognize your value and don't sell yourself short. The price of your course, book, lesson plans, or app shouldn't be based on how long the thing took you to make, but on how long it would take your customers to find the same information and make it themselves. If everything you are teaching is pulled right from Wikipedia, the value is lower than if you are providing your own expertise and wisdom. *You* are what adds value. It can seem daunting to ask for more, but your work is worth it. People understand you've earned this price for your knowledge and experiences.

Finally, my third piece of advice for getting started as a Teacherpreneur is to avoid treating everything equally. This is by far one of my biggest mistakes throughout my business journey. In fact, as soon as I stopped treating everything the same *my business grew 4560%*. Yes, you read that correctly. No, that was not a typo.

Make sure you're focusing on the things that can bring you epic results. Consider the Pareto Principle: 20% of the things you do are responsible for 80% of your success. In business terms:

- 20% of your products bring in 80% of your income

- 20% of your customers generate 80% of your revenue

- 20% of your day-to-day tasks are responsible for 80% of your success

Stop treating everything the same. Just because you have 52 products doesn't mean you need to spend equal time promoting them all. Start with an 80:20 analysis of your business and determine the *right* things to focus on. There are many tasks you're doing now that you could stop without much impact on your business. Be ruthless in searching for the core 20%. Your business will thank you.

You don't have control over everything. If you desire to learn everything first-hand and 'Do It All Yourself' that might be killing your growth. It might seem economical to learn to edit your own images in

Photoshop, but you'll likely spend an absurd amount of time gaining a basic level of proficiency in something you could have hired someone to do without much expense. Stop trying to be everything.

If you have too much to do but can't afford to hire someone, there are two possible scenarios occurring.

Scenario 1:

1. Let's say you want to learn how to edit your own videos.

2. You buy a course, invest in expensive software, and get started becoming proficient enough to make a promo video for your business. At this stage you've invested $500 on the course and software and 25 hours of your own time making it happen.

3. You produce your video and it's OK quality.

Scenario 2:

1. Hire a skilled freelancer on a website like Upwork or Fiverr.

2. Outline what you want done and pay for the video editor's time to complete it for you

3. You receive your video, which is of a much higher quality than you could have ever done, and it only cost you $200. Add in the sales from the new product you just created and pretty soon the decision to focus on the right things becomes much clearer.

While this might seem counter-intuitive, it's the reason the world's largest companies got so big in the first place. At some point the founders realised they couldn't do everything themselves. Many mistakes can be avoided with some forethought and care

CHAPTER 17

Conclusion

One of the most common questions people ask me is: "Why aren't more teachers doing this?"

I get this question from seasoned Teacherpreneurs, incredulous these tactics haven't caught on in the mainstream. "It works so well," they tell me. "Why aren't more people doing it?"

I also get the question from new Teacherpreneurs, skeptical none of their colleagues are engaging in these practices. "If it works so well," they ask, "why aren't more people doing it?"

I honestly don't know the answer. Maybe people are lazy. Or maybe they don't want more responsibility. Maybe it just takes large institutions a long time to change anything—and the education system is a huge institution.

Something similar happened in the 1970's, when David Hancocks, director of Seattle's Woodland Park Zoo, realized that zoos around the world were treating animals in the same devastating way: by putting them into concrete boxes and expecting them to go on living their normal lives as if nothing was wrong. These tactics resulted in animals displaying open signs of boredom and depression, notably the gorillas, who would even go as far as smearing their own feces across the wall— just for something to do. David wanted to change the system, but he didn't know where to start.

"I came to the conclusion that there's no way to close zoos down," he said decades later. Instead, he decided to join the zoos and work to change them from the inside. He looked for a natural setting to house the gorillas. However, no zoo in the world had anything close to what he was looking for. He was faced with a fork in the road: allow things to remain the same or change the way zoos operated. He chose the latter.

After hearing gorilla expert Dian Fossey was coming to the United States, David got in touch with her and set up a meeting in Seattle to see if she could help him conceive of a better design for a gorilla habitat. On the drive back to Seattle's airport, she pointed to the side of the freeway where thick brush and trees grew lush and green.

"That, right there," she said, "is where I would expect to see gorillas in the wild if any lived around here."

Over the next few months, Hancocks and his team, along with some landscape architects, created the world's first natural zoo exhibit. They gave their gorillas a wild area full of trees, rivers, fast-growing plants, and other natural elements. Outsiders worried the gorillas might hurt themselves in their new habitat, but instead, the experiment was a rousing success and zoos around the world started building natural habitats for their animals too.

What happens when you flip convention on its head? What happens when you do the whole thing differently? What happens when you take the market as it is and say, "I think it can be better"?

I'll admit, I've never been a big fan of tradition. Complacency is one big reason we have problems moving forward and pushing the envelope. Change is good, but it's painful. It requires changemakers to bring progress about.

I'm not writing this book to get rich. And I'm not naive enough to think I'm going to change the world either. I am writing to reach *you* in the concrete box of your life and tell you there is another way. You can keep going through the same motions or bring that spark back and reinvigorate your world. What happens when you introduce excitement to your life? The power to do so is within your grasp.

Over the course of this book, I've covered many ways for teachers to make a profit on the side utilizing the skills you already possess. You are a natural communicator, bridging the gaps between students of all ages. You are able to draw out the inherent talents of students around you, build connections with people you have only just met, and make learning exciting. You are an improviser, able to bring concepts and ideas together in ways you never planned. Be brave and look into yourself.

Millenia ago, Sparta existed as a Grecian city-state in the south of the country. Athens, to the East, boasted mighty buildings (which still stand to this day) and massive temples to the gods (which rose above the city like palaces). Sparta didn't roll that way. In fact, the city had no walls. Foreigners were almost dared to come try and take the city. Yet, nobody wanted to, due to the mythical fighting prowess the inhabitants boasted.

Sparta was not known for its beauty, but instead for its military, legendary across the ancient world and immortalized in films like *300*. Few sought to challenge the Spartans, but Phillip II of Macedon was one of those special individuals. He sent a message to the city, the last corner of Greece he'd not yet conquered, inquiring whether to come as friend or foe.

"Neither," was the reply.

Furious, Phillip reached out again with a threat: Surrender, for "if I bring my army onto your land, I will destroy your farms, slay your people, and raze your city."

Sparta, again, sent back one word. "If."

Just like that, Phillip left the city alone. Years later, his son, Alexander the Great, began his siege of the ancient world. He conquered as far as he could, never losing a war, before finally dying of illness. Alexander spread his arm across the entire known world—all except for one small city-state in southern Greece.

While you are probably not a warlord (I hope), you can still learn many fundamental lessons through observing the ancient Spartans. In Sparta every man, woman, and child within the city walls was trained and ready to fight to defend their home. The city acted as an extension of the self and Spartans would die to save their brothers and sisters and the place they loved. They were sure of themselves, even in the face of overwhelming challenges.

The warrior city also knew the power of words (OK, this is a stretch, but I like the story and you already made it to the conclusion, so I doubt you're going to stop reading now no matter what I say). When Phillip sent his blustering messages, Sparta responded with single-word answers. They spoke with abolute clarity and parsimony. Effective communication isn't about talking a lot. In fact, sometimes silence can speak louder than words. Be clear on what you want to say, and make sure you are understood. Then stop talking.

Understand this is not going to be easy. Your journey forward will require bravery. However, others have gone this way and are eager to help you get started. My mother once told me a parable about an old man who swam across a raging river that had taken the lives of many villagers. As soon as he got to the other side he immediately chopped down some nearby trees and began to build a bridge. When people from the town saw him at work they said "old man, you won't be able to build that bridge in your lifetime! It won't be done until after you have passed away!"

The old man turned to them. "Friends," he said, "I swam across the river. I knew the tricks to navigate the water, how to breathe, and how to swim strong. In the future, though, there will be a young man who does not know these things. I do not build this bridge for me, I build this bridge for him."

The journey forward requires courage but I and many others have walked this way before. Let this book serve as your bridge across the river. What I ask is that you continue to strengthen the bridge with the new knowledge you have learned.

Now that we have reached the end, I would like to loop all the way back around to the beginning: Dung beetles. Yeah, you forgot about those little turd bugs, didn't you? Well, dung beetles (whether or not they are wearing cardboard hats) remain one of the most interesting creatures in the world. What would the world look like without them?

Imagine they did not exist. Their chief role, devouring, burying, and distributing all the dung produced by animals around the world, would not be supplemented or replaced by any other animal in the ecosystem (who else would want to do that gross job?). Some animals would adapt better than others, but think about how gross National Geographic would look if all the animals were slogging through fields of their own feces (too late, it's the conclusion, I'm just typing whatever pops into my head, you can't stop me now!). That would be terrible.

Yet, when we think of our favorite animals, we never think about the dung beetles. Lions, elephants, tigers, and apes with different colored bottoms get all the glory. They take up the most Discovery Channel screen time and they have fun adventures involving singing warthogs. Yet, where would all of us be without the dung beetle? Those little troopers put up with a lot of crap.

Friend, I hate to say it, but in this case, you are the dung beetle. You are the one who paves the way for the next generation of people going forward. As a teacher, you have one of the most important roles in society. You educate the next generation. You clear the savannah of all the dung that gets into their heads. When you cross the river, you turn around and start building that bridge to take everyone else along with you. Many are satisfied getting across for themselves, but you have chosen to be the unsung hero of the world. We're in this together and I'm proud to stand with you in this endeavor.

However, teachers are underpaid and underappreciated. Around the world, funding is being stripped from classrooms. Society is willing to take money away from PE, field trips, and the arts, the very practices that show us why life is worth living. This book is not a rallying cry against the system. This is a shot of hope in a very dark room, that you will be able to push on and enjoy the wonderful task you've chosen to undertake.

The most important lesson underscored throughout these pages is that everything you need to achieve success is already at your disposal. Public speaking is just lecturing to a room of hundreds rather than dozens. Tutoring is just individualized teaching. eBooks and online courses are just ways to convey information on the internet. You have these abilities within you already.

I was a PE teacher who started a blog. Now, I am the PE Geek, and I help teachers like you to become Teacherpreneurs. I needed a push to get myself out the door. If you're looking for a sign, here's yours. Thank you for coming on this ride with me. I can't wait to read your book, take your course, purchase your lesson plans, and join your membership program.

CPSIA information can be obtained
at www.ICGtesting.com
Printed in the USA
LVHW051222141020
668673LV00006B/657